Following the Footsteps of

Rabbi Jesus

INTO THE COURTS OF HEAVEN

Study Guide

DESTINY IMAGE BOOKS BY DR. FRANCIS MYLES

*Dangerous Prayers from the Courts of Heaven That Destroy Evil
Altars: Establishing the Legal Framework for Closing Demonic
Entryways and Breaking Generational Chains of Darkness*

*Issuing Divine Restraining Orders from the Courts of Heaven:
Restricting and Revoking the Plans of the Enemy* (with Robert Henderson)

*Following the Footsteps of Rabbi Jesus into the Courts of Heaven:
Partnering with Jesus to Pray Prayers That Hit the Mark*

Following the Footsteps of

Rabbi Jesus

INTO THE COURTS OF HEAVEN

Partnering with Jesus to Pray Prayers that Hit the Mark

 *Study Guide*

Dr. Francis Myles

DESTINY IMAGE® PUBLISHERS, INC.
P.O. Box 310, Shippensburg, PA 17257-0310

"Publishing cutting-edge prophetic resources to supernaturally empower the body of Christ"

This book and all other Destiny Image and Destiny Image Fiction books are available at Christian bookstores and distributors worldwide.

For more information on foreign distributors, call 717-532-3040.

Reach us on the Internet: www.destinyimage.com.

ISBN 13 TP: 978-0-7684-7559-3

ISBN 13 eBook: 978-0-7684-7560-9

For Worldwide Distribution, Printed in the U.S.A.

1 2 3 4 5 6 7 8 / 27 26 25 24 23

Contents

Introduction

Following the Footsteps of Rabbi Jesus into the Courts of Heaven Study Guide is designed to help you delve deeper into the Courts of Heaven, bringing you ever so close to your Savior Jesus Christ and your Advocate, the Holy Spirit. Based on the thirteen chapters in the book of the same name, each page of this study guide ushers you not only into the Courts of Heaven but into your mind, spirit, and soul—revealing your innermost joys and fears, victories and vices, passions and predicaments.

The book as well as this study guide examine and trace the footsteps of Jesus while He lived on earth as a Man, subject to the Law of Moses and the writings of the Prophets, while simultaneously pointing to a time in the very near future when the tension between the Law of Moses, the writing of the Prophets, and the grace of the Lord Jesus Christ would be totally reconciled and fulfilled in Him.

According to Revelation 12:10, in the backdrop is the malicious one who accuses us day and night before the Courts of Heaven. The book and this study guide demonstrate why understanding the symbiotic relationship between the Law of Moses and the grace of our Lord Jesus Christ is critical to living a life of limitless breakthrough.

Following the Footsteps of Rabbi Jesus into the Courts of Heaven and this study guide teach you how to operate effectively in the Courts of Heaven to receive answers to many of your unanswered prayers, while defending your God-given destiny against satan's accusations!

Before you begin this deep dive into Jesus' role in the heavenly courts, I encourage you to pray for clear understanding and godly wisdom—that you will see everything the Lord promises you, and you will learn of His justice, discover His love for you, become the person He created you to be, and live in the freedom Christ died to give you.

When you follow in Rabbi Jesus' footsteps daily, you will be led into amazing adventures, exciting escapades, as well as peaceful pauses in life when you know that you know He is right beside you! Take time to consider each question and scenario, listen for His still, small voice, and then write whatever flows from you. Trust His timing and His faithfulness.

And as you travel along in life with Him, always remember:

Therefore there is now no condemnation [no guilty verdict, no punishment] for those who are in Christ Jesus [who believe in Him as personal Lord and Savior]. For the law of the Spirit of life [which is] in Christ Jesus [the law of our new being] has set you free from the law of sin and of death (Romans 8:1-2 AMP).

Yours for Messiah's Kingdom,
Dr. Francis Myles
Senior Pastor, Dream Genesis Church International
Founder, Francis Myles International

Getting the Most Out of the Study Guide

It is strongly recommended that you work through this study guide in conjunction with the corresponding book. The study is effective as an individual experience or as part of a small group or class.

This resource, a type of *guided journal,* is meant to expand your understanding of Rabbi Jesus' teachings while on earth regarding the Courts of Heaven—His role, the enemy's role, and your role in those courts. You are encouraged to absorb each of the Scriptures, read the excerpts from the book with an open heart and mind, and then thoughtfully answer the questions and consider the scenarios honestly.

Next comes the *Scripture Study and Soul Searching* section that provides relevant verses from the Bible. The Holy Spirit will bring to light new insights that may have been hidden until this very time, growing your faith verse by verse. You are encouraged to write down all that He is revealing to you as you read God's Word.

The *Activation Application* is designed to bring alive what you've learned with practical steps to take in your everyday life—at home, work, church, and with family, friends, coworkers, acquaintances in every sphere. Activating your faith will always refresh, renew, and revitalize you, preparing you to effectively engage in every circumstance for every victory. With each step you take, you move nearer to your God-given destiny and purpose.

Reflections and Ruminations is a place and time to sit back, relax, and allow the Holy Spirit's still, small voice to speak to your spirit all that He wants you to know. Open your mind and heart to what He's saying and you will serenely welcome the soothing peace and joy and comfort that come only from the Prince of Peace, the Good Shepherd, and your heavenly Father. Let yourself sink into the comfy cozy arms of Love—and when you're ready, write about it.

Each session concludes with *Prayers and Proclamations,* directing your attention toward Heaven and the God who answers your prayers and takes serious notice of your proclamations. With Jesus as your best Role Model of a pray-er, you will quickly realize how praying is your direct link to God the Father, placing you before Him not only in the Courts of Heaven but in His house where He welcomes you with open arms.

Then before you turn to the following session, I strongly suggest that you allow the Holy Spirit to bring to the surface any and all thoughts, feelings, ideas, emotions, beliefs, opinions, attitudes, and reactions that were stirred up. Write down and fill up the blank pages and journal space with whatever pops into your mind, heart, spirit.

This study is not intended to simply provide you with information—it is presented to you as a way for you to unlock your destiny in the Courts of Heaven. After all, the more you learn about how the Courts of Heaven work, the more you are able to follow in the footsteps of Rabbi Jesus that always lead toward your heavenly Father.

Jesus: The Rabbi with Authority

And so it was, when Jesus had ended these sayings, that the people were astonished at His teaching, for He taught them as one having authority, and not as the scribes (Matthew 7:28-29 NKJV).

In the cultural setting and time when Jesus launched His ministry, there were a multitude of rabbinical schools and rabbis. However, there also were rabbis who were in a class of their own known as rabbis "with authority." A rabbi with authority was the only one who could introduce new and fresh perspectives on the Law of Moses and the writings of the prophets. All the other rabbis had to tread a narrow and established dogma of the Law of Moses or the unique interpretations of the rabbis with authority.

In Matthew 7:28-29, the orthodox Jews who were listening to Rabbi Jesus were not just astonished at His miracles, they were *"astonished at His teaching."* What was so astonishing about His teaching? Matthew 7:29 gives us insight into the people's perception of Rabbi Jesus' teaching: *"for He taught them as one having authority, and not as the scribes."*

Jesus, the Rabbi with ultimate *semikhah*.

The arrival of the Son of God on earth had been planned by the Father for thousands of years. So, in testifying to the fact that Rabbi Jesus was a rabbi with *semikhah*, God chose the testimony of a very well-respected Jewish prophet and Levitical priest, John the Baptist. It was John the Baptizer who gave a resounding testimony of the loftiness of Rabbi Jesus being the Rabbi with ultimate *semikhah*.

> *John answered them, saying, "I baptize with water, but there stands One among you whom you do not know. It is He who, coming after me, is preferred before me, whose sandal strap I am not worthy to loose." These things were done in Bethabara beyond the Jordan, where John was baptizing. The next day John saw Jesus coming toward him, and said, "Behold! The Lamb of God who takes away the sin of the world! This is He of whom I said, 'After me comes a Man who is preferred before me, for He was before me.' I did not know Him; but that He should be revealed to Israel, therefore I came baptizing with water." And John bore witness, saying, "I saw the Spirit descending from heaven like a dove, and He remained upon Him"* (John 1:26-32 NKJV).

This was a very resounding testimony by a prophet who was feared by both great and small in Israel. Most importantly, John the Baptist was also well known as a rabbi with *semikhah*. Consequently, for a rabbi like John the Baptist with *semikhah* to say that he was not even worthy to untie the straps on Rabbi Jesus' sandals was a huge endorsement. The heavenly Father wanted to make sure that everybody in Israel knew that Rabbi Jesus was the Rabbi with divine *semikhah*. He wanted them to know that as a Rabbi with *semikhah*, Rabbi Jesus had the spiritual authority to interpret the Law of Moses and the writings of the prophets in a manner never seen or heard before:

Now Jesus was telling the disciples a parable to make the point that at all times they ought to pray and not give up and lose heart, saying, "In a certain city there was a judge who did not fear God and had no respect for man. There was a [desperate] widow in that city and she kept coming to him and saying, 'Give me justice and legal protection from my adversary.' For a time he would not; but later he said to himself, 'Even though I do not fear God nor respect man, yet because this widow continues to bother me, I will give her justice and legal protection; otherwise by continually coming she [will be an intolerable annoyance and she] will wear me out.'" Then the Lord said, "Listen to what the unjust judge says! And will not [our just] God defend and avenge His elect [His chosen ones] who cry out to Him day and night? Will He delay [in providing justice] on their behalf?" (Luke 18:1-7 AMP)

I have been tremendously blessed by the understanding that the Lord has given me on the Courts of Heaven through personal encounters with Him. However, I know there are sincere men and women of God who represent a portion of the body of Christ who are standing on the fence concerning embracing the revelation of operating in the Courts of Heaven. The hesitancy in many of these Christ-loving believers was that they could not see how Jesus fit into the whole discussion of the Courts of Heaven. I have learned much from Rabbi Jesus as He single-handedly operated and functioned in this judicial dimension of the Kingdom of God.

Introspection Questions and Scenarios

Where do you "stand" regarding this important piece of your spiritual life?

_____

_____

_____

_____

_____

_____

Rabbi Jesus is the ultimate Rabbi with authority (*semikhah*), with a divine mandate to help you understand how the Kingdom of God operates in the earthly realm. That said, have you encountered someone(s) who taught as having authority? How did you know that person(s) was teaching from a godly spirit?

_____

_____

_____

_____

_____

_____

After reading Luke 18:1-7 and asking the Holy Spirit for His revelation of the passage, write what comes to your spirit, heart, and mind:

_____

_____

_____

_____

_____

_____

As a Christ-loving believer, are you still hesitant to see how Jesus fits into the whole discussion of the Courts of Heaven? Or are you convinced of Jesus' role in standing before the Courts of Heaven? Explain your reasoning.

_____

_____

_____

_____

_____

_____

_____

Scripture Study and Soul Searching

Prayerfully consider each of the following Scriptures relevant in this session and write your thoughts regarding Rabbi Jesus and His authority:

Revelation 12:10

_____

_____

_____

_____

_____

_____

Romans 8:19

_____

_____

_____

_____

_____

_____

Matthew 17:5

_____

_____

_____

_____

_____

_____

Daniel 7:25-26

_____

_____

_____

_____

_____

_____

_____

John 1:17

_____

_____

_____

_____

_____

_____

_____

_____

Matthew 5:17

_____

_____

_____

_____

_____

_____

_____

_____

Romans 6:14

_____

_____

_____

_____

_____

_____

_____

_____

Exodus 20:3

_____

_____

_____

_____

_____

_____

_____

_____

Romans 8:1-2

_____

_____

_____

_____

_____

_____

_____

_____

Matthew 7:28-29

_____

_____

_____

_____

_____

_____

_____

Matthew 18:16

_____

_____

_____

_____

_____

_____

_____

_____

John 1:26-32

_____

_____

_____

_____

_____

_____

_____

_____

Matthew 3:16-17

---

1 John 5:9

Luke 18:1-7

Activation Application

How "cooperative" are you with people in authority? Do you readily and easily submit to authority? Ask your spouse or a trusted friend or coworker how they see you in regard to interacting with authority figures.

_____

_____

_____

_____

_____

_____

At work?

_____

_____

_____

_____

_____

_____

_____

At home?

_____

_____

_____

_____

_____

_____

At church?

_____

_____

_____

_____

_____

_____

If submission doesn't come easily, what actions can you take to react appropriately with people placed in authority over you?

_____

_____

_____

_____

_____

_____

_____

As Jesus is the Rabbi with ultimate authority, or *semikhah,* what are some ways you can honor His authority when you:

Pray

_____

_____

_____

_____

_____

_____

Interact with others

_____

_____

_____

_____

_____

_____

Are facing challenges

_____

_____

_____

_____

_____

_____

_____

Reread the story about the widow who wanted legal justice from the ungodly judge:

> One day Jesus told his disciples a story to show that they should always pray and never give up. "There was a judge in a certain city," he said, "who neither feared God nor cared about people. A widow of that city came to him repeatedly, saying, 'Give me justice in this dispute with my enemy.' The judge ignored her for a while, but finally he said to himself, 'I don't fear God or care about people, but this woman is driving me crazy. I'm going to see that she gets justice, because she is wearing me out with her constant requests!'" Then the Lord said, "Learn a lesson from this unjust judge. Even he rendered a just decision in the end. So don't you think God will surely give justice to his chosen people who cry out to him day and night? Will he keep putting them off?" (Luke 18:1-7 NLT).

With this example in mind that Jesus used in His teaching, write a similar scenario, including dialogue, that you envision between you and your heavenly Judge depicting the same situation. Write every detail that comes to you.

Reflections and Ruminations

Take time to think back to the teachings you've heard over the years, or even most recently. Who immediately came to mind? Write why this person stood out to you. Did the person teach with authority? What type of authority? God-given? Ego-driven? Personality-driven? Others?

_____

_____

_____

_____

_____

_____

_____

_____

_____

_____

_____

What was your response to this person's teaching? Positive? Negative? Why?

_____

_____

_____

_____

_____

_____

_____

_____

_____

_____

_____

The next time you are being taught by or listening to a pastor, minister, Bible study leader, or another, consider the authority under which the person is speaking. Without being judgmental, jot down what comes to your attention—and the takeaway lesson(s).

Session Summary Notes

SESSION 2

The Courts of Heaven Revealed

Now there was a day when the sons of God (angels) came to present themselves before the Lord, and Satan (adversary, accuser) also came among them. The Lord said to Satan, "From where have you come?" Then Satan answered the Lord, "From roaming around on the earth and from walking around on it" (Job 1:6-7 AMP).

The story of lucifer's fall from Heaven as a highly exalted archangel of God permeates both Judaism and traditional Christian teaching. On this one issue there is little or zero variance in doctrine between traditional mainline churches and the more progressive charismatic and Pentecostal churches. The prophetic writings of Ezekiel and Isaiah give us the most vivid front-row seats in the movie of lucifer's fall and his ultimate degeneration into an angel of darkness, capable of incalculable evil!

How you are fallen from heaven, O Lucifer, son of the morning! How you are cut down to the ground, you who weakened the nations! For you have said in your heart: "I will ascend into heaven, I will exalt my throne above the stars of God; I will also sit on the mount of the congregation on the farthest sides of the north; I will ascend above the heights of the clouds, I will be like the Most High." Yet you shall be brought down to Sheol, to the lowest depths of the Pit. Those who see you will gaze at you, and consider you, saying: "Is this the man who made the earth tremble, who shook kingdoms, who made the world as a wilderness and destroyed its cities, who did not open the house of his prisoners?" (Isaiah 14:12-17 NKJV).

Before his historic fall, lucifer was referred to as the anointed cherub who covered Heaven and the angels under him with the worship of Yahweh. He was a one-angel music orchestra until he conceived iniquity in his heart through pride and unrighteous trade. The fall of lucifer, later known as satan, necessitated the revelation of the Courts of Heaven to the children of God.

You were the anointed cherub who covers; I established you; you were on the holy mountain of God; you walked back and forth in the midst of fiery stones. You were perfect in your ways from the day you were created, till iniquity was found in you. By the abundance of your trading you became filled with violence within, and you sinned; therefore I cast you as a profane thing out of the mountain of God; and I destroyed you, O covering cherub, from the midst of the fiery stones. Your heart was lifted up because of your beauty; you corrupted your wisdom for the sake of your splendor; I cast you to the ground, I laid you before kings, that they might gaze at you (Ezekiel 28:14-17 NKJV).

Rabbi Jesus puts the final death nail in the coffin of lucifer's expulsion from the heavenly Kingdom when He declares, *"I saw Satan fall like lightning from heaven"*

(Luke 10:18 NKJV). This was a statement of fact, not open to debate. Rabbi Jesus made this statement to temper the excitement of His disciples over the act of casting out demons versus having their names written in the Lamb's Book of Life in Heaven (see Revelation 21:27 NKJV). So you can imagine my surprise when I first read the following passage from the book of Job:

One day the members of the heavenly court came to present themselves before the Lord, and the Accuser, Satan, came with them. "Where have you come from?" the Lord asked Satan. Satan answered the Lord, "I have been patrolling the earth, watching everything that's going on." Then the Lord asked Satan, "Have you noticed my servant Job? He is the finest man in all the earth. He is blameless—a man of complete integrity. He fears God and stays away from evil." Satan replied to the Lord, "Yes, but Job has good reason to fear God. You have always put a wall of protection around him and his home and his property. You have made him prosper in everything he does. Look how rich he is! But reach out and take away everything he has, and he will surely curse you to your face!" "All right, you may test him," the Lord said to Satan. "Do whatever you want with everything he possesses, but don't harm him physically." So Satan left the Lord's presence (Job 1:6-12 NLT).

I was stunned into a theological quagmire when I contemplated its serious theological implications.

The Holy Spirit said to me, "Francis, even though lucifer was cast out of Heaven (meaning he lost his residency in Heaven), he nevertheless has access to only one part of Heaven until the consummation of this age of sin. God has given him limited access to the Courts of Heaven."

I was blessed and stunned at the same time. The Lord showed me that no self-respecting judge or judicial system would allow a trial to proceed without first seating both the prosecution and the defense (advocate). Satan is the prosecutor, the one who files charges of sinful behavior against the saints in the Courts of Heaven.

In the Courts of Heaven, the only prosecutor is the tempter himself!

John the revelator clearly captures this aspect of satan's work in Revelation 12:10 (AMP):

Then I heard a loud voice in heaven, saying, "Now the salvation, and the power, and the kingdom (dominion, reign) of our God, and the authority of His Christ have come; for the accuser of our [believing] brothers and sisters has been thrown down [at last], he who accuses them and keeps bringing charges [of sinful behavior] against them before our God day and night."

You may be tempted to ask, "Why would Heaven need a court system in the first place, especially after Jesus paid the price for our sins on the cross?" To answer this question, the Lord said to me, "The death of Jesus for humankind's sins provided a remedy for sins committed; it did not, however, stop the Kingdom of God from being what it has always been—a sovereign government and country founded on righteousness and justice. So no self-respecting government would sit idly by while people continue to break and violate the laws of its country with impunity, even in the name of grace. This is a recipe for anarchy."

After the Holy Spirit led me down this path of thinking, the understanding of the Courts of Heaven became a settled issue! After this, the Holy Spirit said to me, "Francis, now that you understand the Courts of Heaven, I want you to know that satan is an officer of the Courts of Heaven, as both the tempter and prosecutor. He will retain this position until the consummation of the age of sin. Then he and his fallen angels and all the children of disobedience will be cast into the lake of fire and brimstone."

Wow—glory to God! His wisdom exceeds all human comprehension.

Introspection Questions and Scenarios

Considering this excerpt from the book and the author's confession of confusion about satan and his stance before God, have you experienced similar quagmires regarding lucifer and his role?

_____

_____

_____

_____

_____

_____

_____

_____

Have the Scriptures in God's Word brought clarity to your confusion? Has the Holy Spirit brought to mind other aspects of the relationship between God and His fallen angel that cause you to wonder? Explain.

_____

_____

_____

_____

_____

_____

_____

_____

Revelation 12:10 clearly reveals that satan is determined to endlessly accuse and bring charges again God's children—you and me. Based on what you learned through the Holy Spirit and in the book, what actions can you take in response to those accusations and charges?

_____

_____

_____

_____

_____

_____

_____

_____

_____

Jesus says:

> *"I have told you these things, so that in Me you may have [perfect] peace. In the world you have tribulation and distress and suffering, but be courageous [be confident, be undaunted, be filled with joy]; I have overcome the world." [My conquest is accomplished, My victory abiding]* (John 16:33 AMP).

Satan is our tempter and our accuser and prosecutor. From Adam and Eve to believers today, his evil continues to permeate the world. What Scriptures counteract this fact and rather reveal the overcoming power of God and His love? Write all that come to mind, then meditate on each.

_____

_____

_____

_____

_____

_____

_____

In Job 1:8, God boasts about His servant Job. In an honest assessment, can God boast of your godly attributes? List them here, remembering that God sees you through the sacrifice of His Son, Jesus:

_____

_____

_____

_____

_____

_____

_____

Scripture Study and Soul Searching

Prayerfully consider each of the following Scriptures relevant in this session and write your thoughts regarding the Courts of Heaven revealed:

Ezekiel 28:14-17

_____

_____

_____

_____

_____

_____

Isaiah 14:12-17

_____

_____

_____

_____

_____

_____

Luke 10:18

_____

_____

_____

_____

_____

_____

Revelation 21:27

_____

_____

_____

_____

_____

_____

Job 1:6-12

_____

_____

_____

_____

_____

_____

_____

1 John 3:4

_____

_____

_____

_____

_____

_____

_____

Matthew 4:1-3

_____

_____

_____

_____

_____

_____

_____

Jude 1:4

_____

_____

_____

_____

_____

_____

_____

Job 2:1-2

_____

_____

_____

_____

_____

_____

_____

Job 1:8

_____

_____

_____

_____

_____

_____

_____

Activation Application

The story of lucifer's fall from Heaven as a highly exalted archangel of God permeates both Judaism and traditional Christian teaching—even doctrine between traditional mainline churches and the more progressive charismatic and Pentecostal churches.

Do some sleuthing online to discover just how similar Jews and Christians are when it comes to lucifer's fall. You may find some surprising facts! Write your findings here.

_____

_____

_____

_____

_____

_____

Did you wonder, "Why would Heaven need a court system in the first place, especially after Jesus paid the price for our sins on the cross?" Write in your own words your version of the Lord's answer to the author. Does it answer your particular question?

_____

_____

_____

_____

_____

_____

Before reading the book and now as you work through this study guide, did you realize that satan is an officer of the Courts of Heaven? Did you know he is both the tempter and prosecutor? How does this truth change your perspective of the heavenly courts? Take a current (not past or future) self-inventory and write what the accuser may have to present against you in the heavenly courts.

_____

_____

_____

_____

_____

_____

_____

If you wrote any legitimate accusations, what steps can you and will you take to rectify those charges before each is presented before the Judge?

_____

_____

_____

_____

_____

_____

_____

Reflections and Ruminations

Consider and then answer each of the following questions in the context of a worldly courtroom setting. Then consider and answer the second set of questions as pertaining to a spiritual courtroom where the accuser and prosecutor is satan, the Holy Spirit is the defense attorney, Jesus is the Advocate, and God is the Judge.

Were you ever personally involved in a judicial proceeding? (If not, answer according to what you've heard or seen on television, etc.)

_____

_____

_____

_____

_____

Were you the accused or the accuser?

_____

_____

_____

_____

_____

_____

If a criminal trial, was it easy to tell if the accused person was guilty or innocent of the crime?

_____

_____

_____

_____

_____

_____

Was an adequate defense presented?

_____

_____

_____

Was there enough evidence to prove guilt?

_____

_____

_____

Was the judge impartial and fair?

_____

_____

_____

If a conviction, was the sentence reasonable and justified?

_____

_____

_____

Now answer as if you were involved in proceedings in the Courts of Heaven:

Before learning about the heavenly courts, how likely is it that satan presented charges against you?

_____

_____

_____

_____

_____

As the accuser/prosecutor, does he have the legal right to bring you before the Judge?

_____

_____

_____

_____

_____

_____

Do onlookers see you as guilty or innocent?

_____

_____

_____

_____

_____

_____

Who presented your defense?

_____

_____

_____

_____

_____

_____

Was there enough evidence to prove your guilt?

_____

_____

_____

_____

_____

_____

Was the Judge impartial and fair?

_____

_____

_____

_____

_____

_____

If a conviction, was the sentence reasonable and justified?

_____

_____

_____

_____

_____

_____

How far did your Advocate go to present a remedy for your act of disobedience, lawbreaking, sin?

_____

_____

_____

_____

_____

_____

Prayers and Proclamations

Your prayers can absolutely usher you into God's presence in the Courts of Heaven. Upon arriving there, allow the Holy Spirit to guide you into proclaiming Jesus, the One who redeemed you from hell and set you free.

Father in Heaven, I realize that I am guilty of sin as it says in Your Word, *"for all have sinned and fall short of the glory of God"* (Romans 3:23 NKJV). Please forgive me of any and all sins committed in the past, present, and future. I stand on Your promise when You said that I *"may receive forgiveness of sins and an inheritance among those who are sanctified by faith"* in You (Acts 26:18 NKJV). Thank You, Lord, for revealing the Courts of Heaven to me so I can be prepared for the charges and accusations that the evil one throws at me. May I be found "not guilty" because I follow in Your righteous footsteps. Every day of my life, heavenly Father, I will thank You for sending Your Son to earth to make the supreme sacrifice, rescuing me from myself so I can bring You glory and praise. You are so worthy of my worship!

I proclaim that You, Lord, are sitting in judgment over all. No one can rule against You, for You alone are the King of the Kingdom of Heaven— there is no higher court on earth or in Heaven!

I declare that satan can only present cases against the children of God— but God is the sole and final voice of judgment!

I proclaim that lucifer's fall from Heaven rendered him impotent and he will never again rise to any position of greatness, in Jesus' name!

I declare that my name is written in the Lamb's Book of Life in Heaven (see Revelation 21:27) and that my eternal home will be with God the Father, God the Son, and God the Holy Spirit!

Session Summary Notes

The Widow and the Corrupt Judge

Now Jesus was telling the disciples a parable to make the point that at all times they ought to pray and not give up and lose heart, saying, "In a certain city there was a judge who did not fear God and had no respect for man. There was a [desperate] widow in that city and she kept coming to him and saying, 'Give me justice and legal protection from my adversary.' For a time he would not; but later he said to himself, 'Even though I do not fear God nor respect man, yet because this widow continues to bother me, I will give her justice and legal protection; otherwise by continually coming she [will be an intolerable annoyance and she] will wear me out.'" Then the Lord said, "Listen to what the unjust judge says! And will not [our just] God defend and avenge His elect [His chosen ones] who cry out to Him day and night? Will He delay [in providing justice] on their behalf? I tell you that He will defend and avenge them quickly. However, when the Son of Man comes, will He find [this kind of persistent] faith on the earth?" (Luke 18:1-8 AMP).

There are few passages in the Gospels that directly connect the Lord Jesus Christ to the Courts of Heaven as much as the beginning passage in Luke 18. For this reason, we will mine these verses for what they're worth, as well as take a front-row seat as Rabbi Jesus ushers us into the realm of breakthrough prayer, which passes directly through the Courts of Heaven.

Rabbi Jesus unveils the attitude of people who are more likely to get the heavenly court to move—those who are divinely persistent until the Judge rules in their favor. Why should we throw in the towel of defeat in prayer when Rabbi Jesus paid the full price of our redemption by the sacrifice of Himself on the cross? Our heavenly and righteous Judge is moved when we by faith refuse to be denied what is legally ours.

> **Once we discover and effectively operate in the Courts of Heaven, answers to prayers will happen quickly.**

This woman in Jesus' parable wanted the judge to give her justice and legal protection from her adversary. Justice is getting the Court to honor and acknowledge the rightfulness of your legal claim to your inalienable rights or property. When Rabbi Jesus asks the question, *"Will He delay [in providing justice] on their behalf?"* He deals a death blow to the dilemma of unanswered prayer that plagues much of the body of Christ worldwide. He is in essence telling us that once we discover this final court of appeal for prayers that have gone unanswered, our righteous Judge will not allow our much-awaited answers to prayer to be delayed any longer.

Rabbi Jesus declares, *"I tell you that He will defend and avenge them quickly."* By this proclamation He makes it abundantly clear that once God's children discover and begin to effectively operate in the Courts of Heaven, answers to prayers will happen quickly.

Key statements that Rabbi Jesus makes in this parable:

1. *"Now Jesus was telling the disciples a parable to make the point that at all times they ought to pray."* Rabbi Jesus forever endorses prayer as the primary modality for communicating with God, as well as securing much-needed answers to prayer. As far as Rabbi Jesus is concerned, every moment we can, we should be found praying.

2. *"They ought to pray and not give up and lose heart."* Rabbi Jesus encourages us not to give up and lose heart. There is a dimension of breakthrough prayer that in faith we must cling to.

3. *"'There was a judge in a certain city,' he said, 'who neither feared God nor cared about people'"* (Luke 18:2 NLT). Rabbi Jesus places prayer within the judicial realm. Rabbi Jesus was referencing the Kingdom of God, which is not a democracy (that requires the separation of powers) but is an autocracy; the eternal Godhead is the executive, legislative, and judiciary of the government of the Kingdom of Heaven. This means that Rabbi Jesus is suggesting a final court of appeal in the heavenly realm for all "unanswered prayers" that require us to approach God as Judge.

4. *"There was a [desperate] widow in that city and she kept coming to him and saying, 'Give me justice and legal protection from my adversary.'"* Rabbi Jesus unveils the attitude of those most likely to get the heavenly court to rule in their

favor. We must be divinely persistent until the heavenly court (Judge) rules in our favor. More so, we can petition our heavenly Father and Judge based on the finished work of Rabbi Jesus on the cross. The widow was not only looking for the restoration of what was legally hers but also for a restraining order from the judge to stop any further infractions by her ruthless adversary. Our heavenly, righteous Judge is moved when we by faith refuse to be denied what is legally ours.

5. *"The judge ignored her for a while, but finally he said to himself, 'I don't fear God or care about people, but this woman is driving me crazy. I'm going to see that she gets justice, because she is wearing me out with her constant requests!'"* (Luke 18:4-5 NLT). Rabbi Jesus shows us the power of the widow's persistence. Our righteous Judge must be convinced of the righteousness of our cause before He will silence the accuser and adversary. Even though the corrupt and unrighteous judge was initially reluctant, he always knew that it was within his judicial power and discretion to give her the verdict she requested.

6. *"Then the Lord said, 'Learn a lesson from this unjust judge. Even he rendered a just decision in the end. So don't you think God will surely give justice to his chosen people who cry out to him day and night?'"* (Luke 18:6 NLT). The unrighteous judge in the parable was a mere metaphor for a very robust heavenly judicial system governed by a righteous and benevolent Judge, who will not hesitate to avenge those of His children who are crying day and night for justice and legal protection from our chief adversary, satan. The phrase Rabbi Jesus uses in the parable, *"who cry out to Him day and night,"* is a direct reference to the Courts of

Heaven (see Revelation 12:10), which never close for a recess; they are open *"day and night."* Rabbi Jesus asks the question, *"Will He delay [in providing justice] on their behalf? I tell you that He will defend and avenge them quickly."* Here He deals a death blow to the dilemma of unanswered prayer that plagues much of the body of Christ worldwide. He is, in essence, telling us that once we discover this final court of appeal for prayers that have gone unanswered, God our righteous Judge will not allow our much-awaited answers to prayer to be delayed any longer.

7. *"However, when the Son of Man comes, will He find [this kind of persistent] faith on the earth?"* Everything in God's Kingdom functions by and through faith, including operating in the Courts of Heaven. Rabbi Jesus is telling us that during His second coming, there will be a famine, a lacking, of real and persistent God-moving faith such as the one displayed by the widow before the unrighteous judge. May this poverty of mountain-moving faith not be your portion, in Jesus' name!

Introspection Questions and Scenarios

As suggested in the book, have you asked yourself this question and answered it: "If the legal rights satan was holding on to over my life or bloodline are discovered and dissolved, why would God hesitate in avenging me upon my adversary?"

_____

_____

_____

_____

_____

_____

_____

Of the three powerful tools for silencing the voice of the accuser in the Courts of Heaven—the blood of Jesus, your testimony, not afraid of death—which one has been the most used in your life so far? Which one the least used? And which one do you rarely call upon to silence satan? Why?

_____

_____

_____

_____

_____

_____

_____

Our adversary knows the inner workings of the heavenly court system and knows that God's holiness does not allow Him to ignore sinful behavior. Has your understanding of the Courts of Heaven and God's holiness changed? Consider Isaiah 5:16 (NLT): *"But the Lord of Heaven's Armies will be exalted by his justice. The holiness of God will be displayed by his righteousness"* and Hebrews 12:10 (NLT): *"But God's discipline is always good for us, so that we might share in his holiness."*

_____

_____

_____

_____

_____

_____

_____

Satan does not operate in the Courts of Heaven to bring accusations against unbelievers because these people are already under his total control. His rampages are to deny believers their God-given destiny. Have you been a victim of his evil tactics? What was your response?

_____

_____

_____

_____

_____

_____

_____

Operating in the Courts of Heaven is not a means of getting saved. Salvation of the soul is solely based on accepting the redemptive sacrifice of Jesus and making Him Lord of your life. This comforting truth makes a difference in how you view the Judge and the accuser in what way(s)?

_____

_____

_____

_____

_____

_____

_____

Scripture Study and Soul Searching

Prayerfully consider each of the following Scriptures relevant in this session and write your thoughts regarding the widow and the corrupt judge:

Luke 18:1-8

_____

_____

_____

_____

_____

_____

1 Peter 5:8

_____

_____

_____

_____

_____

_____

_____

Luke 22:31

_____

_____

_____

_____

_____

_____

Ephesians 4:27

_____
_____
_____
_____
_____
_____

1 John 1:9

_____
_____
_____
_____
_____
_____

Psalm 121:4

_____
_____
_____
_____
_____
_____

Hebrews 11:6

_____

_____

_____

_____

_____

_____

_____

Revelation 12:10-11

_____

_____

_____

_____

_____

_____

_____

_____

Activation Application

Ask the Holy Spirit for wisdom and then rewrite Luke 18:1-8 in your own words (review this passage in several different Bible versions for additional insights).

_____

_____

_____

_____

_____

_____

_____

_____

_____

_____

_____

_____

_____

_____

_____

Sometimes our adversary comes in human flesh. The next time you are confronted by an accuser, before responding:

Call on the precious blood of Jesus, which includes:

_____

_____

_____

_____

_____

Present your testimony to the accuser, saying:

_____

_____

_____

_____

_____

_____

_____

Be confident that you will die to self in obedience to God and, if necessary, die physically rather than deny that Christ is your Savior. How committed are you to these courses of action?

_____

_____

_____

_____

_____

_____

_____

_____

Reflections and Ruminations

Reflecting about the widow who was asking for justice and legal protection, what scenario comes to mind when reading Luke 18:1-8? Was she being harassed by a debt collector? By a man who was taking advantage of her physically, financially, other? Perhaps another woman was jealous of her and was slandering her within the community. Maybe:

_____

_____

_____

_____

_____

_____

When someone nags at you over and over, what is your first reaction?

_____

_____

_____

_____

_____

_____

What is your long-term reaction when the same person continues to nag at you?

_____

_____

_____

_____

_____

_____

Is your reaction to nagging different when it involves (write your reasoning):

An adult

A child

Your spouse

Your boss

A parent

A pastor/teacher

Make it a point to pray every day at the same time—perhaps at 6 o'clock in the morning and 6 o'clock in the evening for six minutes. Pray for the person(s) who happens to be near you at the time. If alone, pray for the person who immediately comes to mind. After all, Rabbi Jesus told His disciples *that all times they ought to pray.*

Prayers and Proclamations

Your prayers can absolutely usher you into God's presence in the Courts of Heaven. Upon arriving there, allow the Holy Spirit, your Advocate, to guide you into proclaiming Jesus, the One who redeemed you from hell and set you free.

My Father in Heaven, I stand before You as a sinner redeemed by the blood of my Savior, Jesus Christ. May my prayer and my life be pleasing in Your sight—thank You for seeing me through the cross. Only with Your faithfulness, grace, and mercy can I pray and not give up and lose heart. Your presence keeps me motivated to march forward, following in the footsteps of Jesus into the Courts of Heaven. There I know I will find justice from a just God. Even the widow in Jesus' story found justice and legal remedy from a callous judge—I know I will find much more because You are a merciful Judge who overrules every injustice.

I proclaim victory in every case brought before the Judge who loves me!

I declare breakthrough in what I seem to think are unanswered prayers, in Jesus' name!

I proclaim the time is now for me to stand strong for the cause of Christ before friends and foes!

I declare that satan will be defeated every time he brings charges against me!

Dear heavenly Judge, Creator, Healer, Provider, Ancient of Days, Avenger, Alpha and Omega, Everlasting Father, Friend, God Almighty, King of kings and Lord of lords, I come to praise You and worship You and nag You. I want to speak to You through prayer so much that Your ears get tired of hearing my voice. I yearn to be ever present near You, so much so that You trip over me every time You take a step. May You see that my heart is pure in my love for You and that I bring a smile to Your face when You think of me. I say as in Deuteronomy 10:21, *"You alone are my God, the only One who is worthy of my praise, the One who has done mighty miracles that I have seen with my own eyes."* And as John the revelator wrote, *"You are worthy, O Lord our God, to receive glory and honor and power. For you created all things, and they exist because you created what you pleased."* In Jesus' name, which is above all names, amen.

Session Summary Notes

Court Is in Session

My dear children, I am writing this to you so that you will not sin. But if any-one does sin, we have an advocate who pleads our case before the Father. He is Jesus Christ, the one who is truly righteous (1 John 2:1 NLT).

According to 1 John 2:1, Rabbi Jesus is our "Advocate." An advocate is a defense attorney, someone who defends and advocates for the rights of the accused in the hopes of securing an acquittal (clearing, release) from the charges (accusations) filed by the prosecution. When it comes to the Courts of Heaven, Rabbi Jesus is not the accuser—He is our faithful Advocate.

The Courts of Heaven are biased in our favor.

No matter how much a believer sins, Rabbi Jesus will never be the accuser. This is not to say that the Lord Jesus winks at our sinful behavior. It grieves His heart more than we know when we sin. No one knows the deadliness of sin like the One who was sacrificed to deliver us from it! Nevertheless, Rabbi Jesus' job is to advocate for our forgiveness and ultimate restoration—not our condemnation. Some legalistic churches, in their desire to justify their hardcore stance on holiness, have transformed both Rabbi Jesus and the Holy Spirit into accusers of the believers. While the call for believers to live a holy life is biblical and noble, we can never make this the

justification for making Rabbi Jesus or the Holy Spirit do the work of the accuser, satan.

Then the guiding angel showed me Joshua the high priest [representing disobedient, sinful Israel] standing before the Angel of the Lord, and Satan standing at Joshua's right hand to be his adversary and to accuse him (Zechariah 3:1 AMP).

Zechariah 3:1 presents us with a face of the heavenly court that we are quite familiar with. This is because this face is eerily similar to the face or dispositions of earthly judicial systems. We quickly see five familiar characters we normally encounter in earthly courts: (1) the accused; (2) the defense attorney; (3) the accuser or prosecutor; (4) the presiding judge; (5) other officers of the court.

The Accused (Defendant): In both the heavenly and earthly realms trials cannot proceed without someone being accused (charged). Regardless of whether the accusation is true or not, accusations bring hurt, suspicion, and the like. Even though you know you're innocent, the sting of the accusation is enough to place you on defense.

The Defense Attorney (Advocate) is represented by the Angel of the Lord (in Zechariah 3:1), an Old Testament reference to Messiah. Even when the defendant (the accused) is guilty, it's the duty of the advocate to deliver the best defense possible. This is the prevailing spirit and attitude of the Advocate Rabbi Jesus in Luke 22:31-32 (NLT), when He declares, *"Simon, Simon, Satan has asked to sift each of you like wheat. But I have pleaded in prayer for you."*

The Prosecutor (Accuser), represented by satan, maintains his adversarial relationship with the accused within the court. The accuser or prosecutor's goal is to deliver a guilty verdict on behalf of the state against the accused. This is satan's primary motivation for bringing accusations (charges) against believers.

The Presiding Trial Judge in Zechariah 3:1 is represented by God the Father, the Judge of all the earth. The judge alone embodies the spirit of the court, and when the presiding judge is seated court is in session, as in "the seating of the court" (see Daniel 7:10). The beautiful thing about operating in the Courts of Heaven is that the presiding Judge is our loving heavenly Father!

Other officers of the heavenly court include "scribe angels" who are stewards of the court's oral and written records. Bailiffs are guardians of court protocol. I believe there are bailiff angels that are guardians of the heavenly courts' protocols and enforcers of the courts' righteous judgments.

And the Angel of the Lord [solemnly and earnestly] admonished Joshua, saying, "Thus says the Lord of hosts, 'If you will walk in My ways [that is, remain faithful] and perform My service, then you will also govern My house and have charge of My courts, and I will give you free access [to My presence] among these who are standing here'" (Zechariah 3:6-7 AMP).

Thankfully, the Angel of the Lord (our faithful Advocate) delivers a huge and righteous verdict, favorable to Joshua the high priest. Most people find going to court in the natural quite scary and taxing. However, coming before the heavenly court after the death and resurrection of Rabbi Jesus to silence the voice of the accuser ought to be an exhilarating experience for every believer. The Courts of Heaven are biased in our favor. God wants us to grant Him the legal right He needs to rule in our favor and grant us what Christ has already secured for us.

Introspection Questions and Scenarios

Have you ever been accused by a friend, spouse, or foe of something you never did or said? Was it hard to defend yourself? What was the person's motive for the false accusation? Who was your advocate? If this hasn't been your experience, do you know someone who was falsely accused? How did the person handle it?

_____

_____

_____

_____

_____

_____

_____

_____

Read the entire Scripture passage of Zechariah 3:1-7 from the Amplified Bible. How does this trial scene compare with any you may have been involved in, know someone who has been, or perhaps you watched on television? In what ways does a human judge compare to God the ultimate Judge of the universe?

_____

_____

_____

_____

_____

_____

_____

_____

Two redeeming principles defined in the book:

1. The Lord Jesus (our Advocate) uses the Courts of Heaven to render righteous verdicts on our behalf and has to do with God's commitment to His own predetermined purposes.

2. The Lord Jesus (our Advocate) uses the Courts of Heaven to issue righteous verdicts on our behalf and has to do with the fact that He is our Kinsman Redeemer.

How do God's predetermined purposes affect your life?

_____

_____

_____

_____

_____

_____

_____

What does knowing God is your Kinsman Redeemer mean to you? What type of relationship do you envision?

_____

_____

_____

_____

_____

_____

_____

_____

Scripture Study and Soul Searching

Prayerfully consider each of the following Scriptures relevant in this session and write your thoughts regarding when Court is in session:

1 John 2:1

_____

_____

_____

_____

_____

_____

_____

Zechariah 3:1-7

_____

_____

_____

_____

_____

_____

_____

Luke 22:31-32

_____

_____

_____

_____

_____

_____

_____

Daniel 7:9-10

_____

_____

_____

_____

_____

_____

_____

Daniel 4:31-33

_____

_____

_____

_____

_____

_____

_____

Zechariah 3:3-5

_____

_____

_____

_____

_____

_____

_____

Matthew 15:19

_____

_____

_____

_____

_____

_____

_____

Isaiah 46:10

_____

_____

_____

_____

_____

_____

_____

James 2:13

_____

_____

_____

_____

_____

_____

_____

Hebrews 12:24

Zechariah 3:6-7

Luke 22:31-32

Luke 22:33-34

_____

_____

_____

_____

_____

_____

_____

John 21:3-4

_____

_____

_____

_____

_____

_____

_____

Daniel 7:9-10

_____

_____

_____

_____

_____

_____

_____

1 Kings 18:24

_____

_____

_____

_____

_____

_____

Psalm 139:15-17

_____

_____

_____

_____

_____

_____

_____

Activation Application

In the passage from Zechariah 3, Joshua was told to change out of his filthy clothes and head covering and to put on clean clothes and turban. The book explains that this act was symbolically removing the filth of sin from Joshua's spirit and mind. Take time to think about anything within and/or outside of you that needs to be shed and replaced with cleansing purity. List whatever comes to mind, then take action.

_____
_____
_____
_____
_____
_____
_____

For out of the heart come evil thoughts and plans, murders, adulteries, sexual immoralities, thefts, false testimonies, slanders (verbal abuse, irreverent speech, blaspheming) (Matthew 15:19 AMP).

How does this Scripture verse differ from what the world says comes "out of the heart"? Such as love, good feelings, and compassion, etc. Give examples.

_____
_____
_____
_____
_____
_____
_____

Reflections and Ruminations

Reflect on the following verses from God's Word in the New and Old Testaments and then write your understanding of the differences between and/or the similarities of your heart and mind.

*You shall love the Lord your God with all your **heart** and **mind** and with all your soul and with all your strength [your entire being]* (Deuteronomy 6:5 AMP).

*And He who searches the **hearts** knows what the **mind** of the Spirit is, because the Spirit intercedes [before God] on behalf of God's people in accordance with God's will* (Romans 8:27 AMP).

*I will bless the Lord who has counseled me; indeed, my **heart (mind)** instructs me in the night* (Psalm 16:7 AMP).

*And the peace of God [that peace which reassures the heart, that peace] which transcends all understanding, [that peace which] stands guard over your **hearts** and your **minds** in Christ Jesus [is yours]* (Philippians 4:7 AMP).

*A happy **heart** is good medicine and a joyful **mind** causes healing, but a broken spirit dries up the bones* (Proverbs 17:22 AMP).

*Come close to God [with a contrite **heart**] and He will come close to you. Wash your hands, you sinners; and purify your [unfaithful] **hearts**, you double-**minded** [people]* (James 4:8 AMP).

Prayers and Proclamations

Your prayers can absolutely usher you into God's presence in the Courts of Heaven. Upon arriving there, allow the Holy Spirit, your Advocate, to guide you into proclaiming Jesus, the One who redeemed you from hell and set you free.

Heavenly Father, Righteous Judge, it is written in Psalm 91:11 (AMP), *"For He will command His angels in regard to you, to protect and defend and guard you in all your ways [of obedience and service]."* I therefore ask You to send high-ranking angelic officers of the Court who excel in strength to execute Your righteous judgment against all demonic entities opposing my relationship with the Holy Spirit, in Jesus' name I pray. I decree and declare that by His stripes, I am healed, in Jesus' name.

Heavenly Father, based on Jesus' finished work and my heartfelt repentance, I now move on the Courts of Heaven to dismiss all of satan's accusations and charges against me and my bloodline, in Jesus' name. For it is written in Revelation 12:10 that the accuser of our believing brothers and sisters has been cast down. So I petition You, heavenly Father, to cast down and nullify all of satan's accusations against me, in Jesus' name I pray.

I proclaim that the blood of Jesus erases every evil decree issued against me and my family!

I declare that every demonic entity attached to evil utterances designed to destroy my finances and prosperity are all cast out of my life now, in Jesus' name!

I proclaim and surrender all rights to self-representation in the Courts of Heaven. Instead I ask the Lord Jesus Christ who is my faithful Advocate to plead for me before You!

I declare and decree that any curse weaponized against me to destroy my life and destiny is ended now in the mighty name of Jesus!

Session Summary Notes

Agreeing with the Adversary

*Therefore if you bring your gift to the altar, and there remember that your brother has something against you, leave your gift there before the altar, and go your way. First be reconciled to your brother, and then come and offer your gift. **Agree with your adversary** quickly, while you are on the way with him, lest your adversary deliver you to the judge, the judge hand you over to the officer, and you be thrown into prison. Assuredly, I say to you, you will by no means get out of there till you have paid the last penny* (Matthew 5:23-26 NKJV).

In the Scripture passage from Matthew 5, Rabbi Jesus is dealing with spiritual offenses that God's people commit at the altar of God. He wants us to know that sins against the altar carry severe consequences in the Courts of Heaven. Giving a tainted offering to the Lord at an altar gives satan legal rights against the giver. For the longest time, I failed to grasp the power of what Rabbi Jesus was suggesting in the phrase *"agree with your adversary."* Thankfully, when the understanding of the Courts of Heaven became a reality in my life, I realized what Rabbi Jesus was suggesting—a legal strategy designed to silence the accuser's voice in the Courts of Heaven.

> ## Giving a tainted offering to the Lord at an altar gives satan legal rights against the giver.

Agreeing with our adversary is neutralizing through acts of heartfelt repentance all the accusations and legal rights satan has against us. Sin, the transgression of the law, is the primary fuel and driver behind all of satan's accusations. More often than not, satan has irrefutable evidence to put us on trial because of unconfessed sin or generational iniquity. Acting as if we haven't sinned or using God's grace to excuse ourselves from taking responsibility for our sin violates Rabbi Jesus' legal strategy (see 1 John 1:9 NKJV).

On the other hand, 1 John 1:9 (AMP) declares, *"If we [freely] admit that we have sinned and confess our sins, He is faithful and just [true to His own nature and promises], and will forgive our sins and cleanse us continually from all unrighteousness [our wrongdoing, everything not in conformity with His will and purpose]."*

This passage of Scripture in 1 John 1:9 contains the full understanding of what Rabbi Jesus meant in Matthew 5:25. He commanded us to agree with our adversary on our way to court so the accuser (satan) cannot prevail against us in the Courts of Heaven once he presents his case against us. So we agree with the adversary when we repent of our sins and allow the blood of Jesus to cleanse us from all unrighteousness.

Come to terms quickly [agree with your adversary] [at the earliest opportunity] with your opponent at law while you are with him on the way [to court], so that your opponent does not hand you over to the judge, and the judge to the guard, and you are thrown into prison. I assure you and most solemnly say to you, you will not come out of there until you have paid the last cent (Matthew 5:25-26 AMP).

Rabbi Jesus sternly warns against the danger of violating or not adhering to His admonition to agree with our adversary before we step into the Courts of Heaven. No matter how much God loves us, if we ignore the principle of agreeing with our chief adversary (satan), we give satan tremendous power against us in the Courts of Heaven.

Rabbi Jesus says that walking in the attitude that we don't have to repent because we are not under the Law but under grace can have disastrous spiritual consequences. When satan has irrefutable evidence of our sinful behavior, it will move the Courts of Heaven in his favor.

We must agree with the adversary and repent of our sins and allow the blood of Jesus to cleanse us from all unrighteousness, which confirms King Solomon's declaration in Proverbs 28:13 (AMP); *"He who conceals his transgressions will not prosper, but whoever confesses and turns away from his sins will find compassion and mercy."*

If we fail to agree with the adversary, our righteous Judge has no choice but to hand us over to the guard (demonic tormentors) who will in turn throw us in "prison" until we have fully paid for our sin. Please remember, the Courts of Heaven are not about personal salvation. The Courts of Heaven are about spiritual contentions of fulfilling our God-given destiny on earth.

The Courts of Heaven are about spiritual contentions of fulfilling our God-given destiny on earth.

Agreeing with the adversary, in addition to heartfelt repentance, has to do with how we handle the daily cares of life. In Matthew 6:34 (NKJV)—*"Therefore do not worry about tomorrow, for tomorrow will worry about its own things. Sufficient for the day is its own trouble"*— Rabbi Jesus warns against worrying, and yet for most of us this is the easiest sin to fall into.

According to 1 Peter 5:7-8, if we fail to *"cast our care"* on Jesus, satan will take advantage of us and use our worries against us. He will devour us like a roaring lion if we fail to stay sober and vigilant by casting our cares, anxieties, worries, and concerns on the Lord Jesus Christ. We must quickly agree with the adversary by saying, "Satan, I refuse to jump into the cesspool of endless worries. Rather, I will cast all my worries and cares on my Lord's big shoulders." This robs our adversary of the spiritual ammunition created by our worrying.

Introspection Questions and Scenarios

So if you are presenting a sacrifice at the altar in the Temple and you suddenly remember that someone has something against you, leave your sacrifice there at the altar. Go and be reconciled to that person. Then come and offer your sacrifice to God. When you are on the way to court with your adversary, settle your differences quickly. Otherwise, your accuser may hand you over to the judge, who will hand you over to an officer, and you will be thrown into prison (Matthew 5:23-25 NLT).

No matter which Bible version you read of this passage in Matthew, the message is loud and clear. Write exactly what the Lord is telling you, and why it is so important to follow His instructions.

_____

_____

_____

_____

_____

If we [freely] admit that we have sinned and confess our sins, He is faithful and just [true to His own nature and promises], and will forgive our sins and cleanse us continually from all unrighteousness [our wrongdoing, everything not in conformity with His will and purpose] (1 John 1:9 AMP).

This passage of Scripture in 1 John 1:9 contains the full understanding of what Rabbi Jesus meant in Matthew 5:25. He commanded us to agree with our adversary on our way to court so the accuser (satan) cannot prevail against us in the Courts of Heaven once he presents his case against us.

Perhaps you haven't thought about agreeing with your adversary in this context. Does it make sense? Do you have doubts about this strategy? Why or why not?

_____

_____

_____

_____

_____

_____

What is the difference between a street-brawling accuser and a slick prosecutor who knows the law? Which would you rather confront in the Courts of Heaven?

_____

_____

_____

_____

_____

_____

If believers ignore the principle of agreeing with satan, our chief adversary, we give him tremendous power against us in the Courts of Heaven. Do you believe that you don't have to repent because you are not under the Law but under grace? How can this belief have disastrous spiritual consequences?

_____

_____

_____

_____

_____

Scripture Study and Soul Searching

Prayerfully consider each of the following Scriptures relevant in this session and write your thoughts regarding agreeing with your adversary:

Matthew 5:23-26

_____

_____

_____

_____

_____

_____

_____

1 John 1:8

_____

_____

_____

_____

_____

_____

1 John 1:9

_____

_____

_____

_____

_____

_____

_____

Proverbs 28:13

_____

_____

_____

_____

_____

_____

_____

1 Peter 5:7-8

_____

_____

_____

_____

_____

_____

_____

Matthew 6:34

_____

_____

_____

_____

_____

_____

_____

Activation Application

Read this familiar Scripture passage: *"So if you are presenting a sacrifice at the altar in the Temple and you suddenly remember that someone has something against you, leave your sacrifice there at the altar. Go and be reconciled to that person. Then come and offer your sacrifice to God"* (Matthew 5:23-24 NLT). Believers are to present themselves daily as a living sacrifice to God; therefore, every day you need to reconcile yourself to anyone who has something against you. Start now by listing people's names and the action you will be taking to rectify the issue:

Reflections and Ruminations

After reflection and moving on to ruminating about the following statements, write what you discover about yourself:

Rather than agreeing with my adversary, I'm more likely to make excuses for my sin.

_____

_____

_____

_____

_____

_____

Rather than agreeing with my adversary, I'd rather ignore any little indiscretion in my life.

_____

_____

_____

_____

_____

_____

Rather than agreeing with my adversary, I will count on God's grace to clean up my mess.

_____

_____

_____

_____

_____

_____

Rather than agreeing with my adversary, I'll turn to my pastor to forgive me.

_____

_____

_____

_____

_____

_____

Rather than agreeing with my adversary, I would rather just sweep it under the rug and pretend it will go away eventually.

_____

_____

_____

_____

_____

_____

_____

Rather than agreeing with my adversary, I can justify it by comparing my minor sin to other people's major sins.

_____

_____

_____

_____

_____

_____

Rather than agreeing with my adversary, I promise never to do it again.

Rather than agreeing with my adversary, I fall into the trap of pride and won't admit my wrongdoing—to myself, others, God.

Rather than agreeing with my adversary, I listen to others who tell me I'm a good person with nothing to feel bad about.

Rather than agreeing with my adversary, I ask someone to pray for me.

_____

_____

_____

_____

_____

_____

_____

As I am preparing to sacrifice myself to God each day, I agree with my accuser that I have sinned. I repent and ask forgiveness from my heavenly Father. And I immediately address the issue with whomever may have something against me.

_____

_____

_____

_____

_____

_____

_____

Prayers and Proclamations

Your prayers can absolutely usher you into God's presence in the Courts of Heaven. Upon arriving there, allow the Holy Spirit, your Advocate, to guide you into proclaiming Jesus, the One who redeemed you from hell and set you free.

Heavenly Father, I know that until the end of the age of sin, satan still has legal access to the Courts of Heaven to level accusations against God's children, including me. Rabbi Jesus declares in Matthew 5:25 (AMP), *"Come to terms quickly [at the earliest opportunity] with your opponent at law while you are with him on the way [to court], so that your opponent does not hand you over to the judge, and the judge to the guard, and you are thrown into prison."* Righteous Judge, in compliance with the admonishment of the Lord Jesus, I choose to quickly agree with all legitimate accusations of my adversary, satan, that he is using to imprison my destiny. I choose to quickly agree with my adversary, satan, so he will no longer manipulate the gates of hell against me, in Jesus' name.

I proclaim that every demonically engineered curse or evil device against me that is connected to the gates of hell is now canceled, in the name of Jesus!

I declare that the blood of Jesus erases every evil decree issued against me, in Jesus' name!

I proclaim that demonic entities attached to evil utterances designed to condemn me to hell are all cast out of my life, now!

I declare that my righteous verdict of release and breakthrough is now secured in the documents of the Courts of Heaven!

Session Summary Notes

SESSION 6

Prison Sentences Imposed by the Courts of Heaven

*Come to terms quickly [at the earliest opportunity] with your opponent at law while you are with him on the way [to court], so that your opponent does not hand you over to the judge, and the judge to the guard, and you are **thrown into prison**. I assure you and most solemnly say to you, you will not come out of there until you have paid the last cent* (Matthew 5:25-26 AMP).

Rabbi Jesus was referencing the tenets of a spiritual and heavenly court in Matthew 5:25-26. What does Rabbi Jesus mean when He boldly declares, *"so that your opponent does not hand you over to the judge, and the judge to the guard, and you are thrown into prison. I assure you and most solemnly say to you, you will not come out of there until you have paid the last cent"*? What does being thrown into prison mean or look like? Since Rabbi Jesus was referencing a spiritual court rather than a natural court, the interpretation has to be spiritual. Most importantly, the offenses Rabbi Jesus is alluding to here are unforgiveness and being offended.

The first thing the Holy Spirit told me was to focus on the word *prison* not as a physical place of incarceration but as a spiritual state of being imprisoned. In this vein of thinking, the Spirit of God told me to analyze the English meanings of the word *prison*. I discovered via an online thesaurus, "Prison by definition is any place of confinement or involuntary restraint." Then the Spirit of God said to me, "Also examine what people in prison cannot do or what they forfeit, and you will start to understand

the picture Rabbi Jesus is communicating about prison sentences imposed by the Courts of Heaven."

Suddenly I saw it! When people are incarcerated, they lose some of their citizenship rights, such as voting in elections and the right to work or run a business. The Holy Spirit showed me that there are many Kingdom citizens who are Heaven-bound, but in their earthly life they are living below what Rabbi Jesus died for on the cross. They are imprisoned by rudimentary elements of this world. Some are serving their spiritual prison sentences in unequally yoked marriages that will never allow them to fulfill their God-given destiny. They spend more time in therapy than basking in the glory of the anointing.

Many believers are imprisoned by rudimentary elements of the world.

Places of imprisonment can include marriages (see the book for a detailed explanation of this unfortunate but true reality) as well as spiritual imprisonment in the house of financial debt. Rabbi Jesus uses the expression *"you will not come out of there until you have paid the last cent"* to describe imprisonment imposed by the Courts of Heaven for failing to reconcile or forgive someone before giving your offering at the altar of the Lord. Rabbi Jesus uses a monetary term "penny" or "cent" to describe this prison, characterized by a long season of financial debt. The guards of this prison are the "creditors." Believers' destinies are under arrested development; every time money to advance in life appears, it quickly disappears into the hands of creditors.

God is the One who created us with the capacity to generate both thought and corresponding action, so He alone is capable of judging both. So it becomes clear that Rabbi Jesus is alluding to the penal code of a spiritual court in Matthew 5:23-26.

Matthew 5:21 ties the action of murder to harboring thoughts of anger against someone, especially a believing brother or sister in Christ. You will notice that under the Mosaic Law, people were only penalized for actual action, not the thoughts that led up to the actual act of homicide. In Matthew 5:27-28, Rabbi Jesus upgrades the Mosaic Law on adultery by tying the action of adultery to thought, not just action.

Grace has higher standards of righteousness than what was required by the Law of Moses.

This means that unlike what most Christians think, grace has higher standards of righteousness than what was required by the Law of Moses. The Law of Moses did not declare anyone guilty of adultery by merely thinking about it. They had to find someone in the very act of adultery in order to prosecute (see John 8). However,

when Rabbi Jesus introduced the Courts of Heaven to the people who lived under the Law, He shocked many of them.

Sickness is another common spiritual house of imprisonment. Based on their Hebraic understanding of sin and consequence, the disciples asked Rabbi Jesus the question, *"Rabbi (Teacher), who sinned, this man or his parents, that he would be born blind?"* (John 9:1-2 AMP). Rabbi Jesus never refuted their theological basis for linking sin with a person's imprisonment in the house of sickness.

> *They brought to Him a man who was paralyzed, lying on a stretcher. Seeing their [active] faith [springing from confidence in Him], Jesus said to the paralytic, "Do not be afraid, son; your sins are forgiven [**the penalty is paid, the guilt removed, and you are declared to be in right standing with God**]"* (Matthew 9:2 AMP).

Matthew 9:2, with theological integrity, clearly concludes that there is an inescapable connection between sin and sickness. Interestingly, in healing the paralyzed man, Rabbi Jesus uses legal terms to describe both the basis of his sickness (paralysis) and the man's emancipation. Rabbi Jesus declares, *"the penalty is paid, the guilt removed, and you are declared to be in right standing with God."* This statement is commuting a prison sentence.

John 9:1-12 tells the story of when Rabbi Jesus healed a blind man. He had been incarcerated in the house of sickness since birth. Think on this! And in John 5:1-15, Jesus healed a man who had been an invalid for thirty-eight years. How many would not wail in anguish if a judge sentenced a loved one to thirty-eight years in prison? I know of mothers who fainted when a lesser sentence than this was passed on their wayward children.

It's not been surprising to see many healings that have taken place in our ministry when we take people into the Courts of Heaven to present their cases. People from around the world who read my books on the Courts of

Prison Sentences Imposed by the Courts of Heaven

Heaven are also being released from their imprisonment in the house of sickness.

Rabbi Jesus warned of a terrifying house of imprisonment known as hell.

Rabbi Jesus, more so than any of the prophets before Him, warned of a very dangerous and terrifying house of imprisonment known as hell (see Matthew 10:28). If anybody knew the absolute horrors of this house of imprisonment of the "unsaved dead" and "apostate believers," it's Rabbi Jesus. He died on the cross to pay for the penalty of sin so that no human being ever has to go to this spiritual torture chamber. Revelation 14:11 gives us a glimpse of what to expect in this terrifying house of imprisonment. The verse ought to make the hairs on your back crawl just thinking about a place where both body and soul have no rest nor peace.

And if you thought hell was a terrifying house of imprisonment, think again! (Read Revelation 20:13-15.) God has a final solution—a place of unimaginable suffering and lamentation for both humans and angels. While hell is a house of imprisonment for the unsaved dead and apostate believers, it's not a place of imprisonment and punishment for the devil and his angels. In hell, satan is the prison warden, and his minions are the prison guards. However, once God initiates the final solution, satan and his angels and the damned in hell will all be cast into the lake of fire and brimstone.

May Rabbi Jesus release you today from being a prisoner in every sense of the word!

Introspection Questions and Scenarios

Have you been sentenced to any spiritual imprisonment houses because of unforgiveness? Unrepentance? Squandering resources? If so, what is your first step to break out of that prison?

_____

_____

_____

_____

_____

_____

_____

_____

_____

Are you being held captive by sickness? Are you being held back from your God-given destiny because of illness? What does it take to declare freedom?

_____

_____

_____

_____

_____

_____

_____

_____

_____

_____

The book *Following the Footsteps of Rabbi Jesus into the Courts of Heaven* goes into detail about the spiritual torture chamber that Rabbi Jesus endured in hell, where the unsaved dead and apostate believers are sent, as well as the final house of imprisonment—the lake of fire, where the devil and his angels will end up.

Are you afraid of being sent to prison by the Courts of Heaven Judge? Why is this an impossible scenario knowing what Jesus did on the cross for you?

Scripture Study and Soul Searching

Prayerfully consider each of the following Scriptures relevant in this session and write your thoughts regarding prison sentences imposed by the Courts of Heaven:

Matthew 5:23-26

_____

_____

_____

_____

_____

_____

Matthew 5:21-22

_____

_____

_____

_____

_____

_____

_____

Matthew 5:27-28

_____

_____

_____

_____

_____

_____

1 Corinthians 6:16

_____

_____

_____

_____

_____

_____

_____

Matthew 19:6

_____

_____

_____

_____

_____

_____

Genesis 6:4

_____

_____

_____

_____

_____

_____

_____

Numbers 13:33

_____

_____

_____

_____

_____

_____

Jude 1:6

_____

_____

_____

_____

_____

_____

2 Kings 4:1-7

_____

_____

_____

_____

_____

_____

_____

John 9:1-2

_____

_____

_____

_____

_____

_____

John 5:5-9

_____

_____

_____

_____

_____

_____

Matthew 9:2-7

_____

_____

_____

_____

_____

_____

Daniel 4:4-8

_____

_____

_____

_____

_____

_____

_____

Daniel 4:9-12

_____

_____

_____

_____

_____

_____

_____

Daniel 4:13-18

_____

_____

_____

_____

_____

_____

Mark 5:14-20

Daniel 4:19

Daniel 4:27

1 John 1:9

_____

_____

_____

_____

_____

_____

_____

Daniel 4:34-37

_____

_____

_____

_____

_____

_____

_____

Matthew 10:28

_____

_____

_____

_____

_____

_____

_____

Revelation 14:11

Revelation 20:13-15

Revelation 20:7-8

Activation Application

In the book *Following the Footsteps of Rabbi Jesus into the Courts of Heaven,* the full story of King Nebuchadnezzar's spiritual imprisonment by the Courts of Heaven is told. His divine judgment came in a very detailed dream that was beyond human or demonic comprehension. All the best magicians and sorcerers in Babylon failed to decipher the dream. Daniel, a believer and an officer of the Courts of Heaven, interpreted the dream. In part, Daniel told the king:

> *Therefore, O king, let my advice be acceptable to you; break off your sins by being righteous, and your iniquities by showing mercy to the poor. Perhaps there may be a lengthening of your prosperity* (Daniel 4:27 NKJV).

To *break off your sins by being righteous* is to offer God your heartfelt repentance. Do that here for any and every sin that comes to your attention:

_____

_____

_____

_____

_____

_____

Daniel also advised the king to *show mercy to the poor.* How merciful are you to those less fortunate? What action(s) can you take today to follow Daniel's advice, which he received from the Lord to tell the king? Make a list and determine to follow up regularly.

_____

_____

_____

_____

_____

_____

_____

Reflections and Ruminations

In the world judicial system, after the offender has served the sentence, the prisoner is released from prison. The Courts of Heaven function in the exact same way, with one major exception. It's a spiritual court where the presiding Judge loves mercy more than judgment.

For example, as soon as King Nebuchadnezzar finished serving out the seven-year sentence imposed on him by the Courts of Heaven for the sin of pride, he was released from his mental imprisonment. He started praising God, and God made people look for him to restore him to the empty throne.

Take to heart the king's story:

> *After this time had passed, I, Nebuchadnezzar, looked up to heaven. My sanity returned, and I praised and worshiped the Most High and honored the one who lives forever. His rule is everlasting, and his kingdom is eternal. All the people of the earth are nothing compared to him. He does as he pleases among the angels of heaven and among the people of the earth. No one can stop him or say to him, "What do you mean by doing these things?" When my sanity returned to me, so did my honor and glory and kingdom. My advisers and nobles sought me out, and I was restored as head of my kingdom, with even greater honor than before. Now I, Nebuchadnezzar, praise and glorify and honor the King of heaven. All his acts are just and true, and he is able to humble the proud* (Daniel 4:34-37 NLT).

How comforting it is to realize that the King of Heaven's acts are just and true, that He forgives all sin when repentance is sincere, and restoration is complete in Him.

Prayers and Proclamations

Your prayers can absolutely usher you into God's presence in the Courts of Heaven. Upon arriving there, allow the Holy Spirit, your Advocate, to guide you into proclaiming Jesus, the One who redeemed you from hell and set you free.

Heavenly Father, righteous Judge, I ask You to forgive me and restore to me all that I allowed to be taken because of my sin. Please seal my righteous verdict and silence the voice of the accuser, in the precious blood of Jesus. May You also cover with the blood of Jesus all my legal proceedings in this Court. Thank You for sealing this breakthrough. Lord, I thank You for all the voices in the Courts of Heaven that are speaking on my behalf. I celebrate the finished work of Your Son, Rabbi Jesus, on the cross of Calvary. I thank You that because of what Rabbi Jesus did, I am redeemed. You triumphed over principalities and powers through the cross and You made them a public spectacle. I receive by faith the spoils of war that You purchased for me through Your suffering, death, and resurrection, in Jesus' name.

I proclaim my righteous verdict of release and breakthrough from the tormenting voice of the accuser!

I declare that in every spiritual battle no internal or external weapon of the enemy formed against me shall prosper!

I proclaim and renounce all generational curses of pride, lust, perversion, rebellion, witchcraft, idolatry, poverty, rejection, fear, confusion, addiction, and death be destroyed in Jesus' name!

I declare that all verbal curses and negative words spoken over me are broken and that the devil has no authority to arrest my destiny!

Session Summary Notes

SESSION 7

Jesus Fulfills the Law of Moses

For the grace of God has been revealed, bringing salvation to all people. And we are instructed to turn from godless living and sinful pleasures. We should live in this evil world with wisdom, righteousness, and devotion to God, while we look forward with hope to that wonderful day when the glory of our great God and Savior, Jesus Christ, will be revealed. He gave his life to free us from every kind of sin, to cleanse us, and to make us his very own people, totally committed to doing good deeds (Titus 2:11-14 NLT).

In my opinion, no other Scripture has been extended beyond its proper biblical boundary more than Romans 6:14. Some teachers in the body of Christ have used Romans 6:14 to create a church culture saturated with the doctrine of "hyper-grace." Under this hyper-grace culture, sin is being entertained and tolerated in the church. I am convinced that many of the accusations in the Courts of Heaven that satan has against many of God's children are connected to the misuse or abuse of God's grace.

I completely agree that New Testament believers are not under the dispensation of law but under grace. I also agree with the spirit of Romans 6:14 that when we are operating accurately under the power of God's true grace, sin will not have dominion or control over our lives.

For the grace of God has been revealed, bringing salvation to all people. And we are instructed to turn from godless living and sinful pleasures. We should live in this evil world with wisdom, righteousness, and devotion to God, while we look forward with hope to that wonderful day when the glory of our great God and Savior, Jesus Christ, will be revealed.

He gave his life to free us from every kind of sin, to cleanse us, and to make us his very own people, totally committed to doing good deeds (Titus 2:11-14 NLT).

According to Titus, the following is an apostolic list of the amazing work of the true grace of God in the human heart:

- The grace of God brings salvation.

- The grace of God has appeared and been made available to all people.

- The grace of God teaches us how to deny ungodliness.

- The grace of God teaches us how to deny worldly lusts.

- The grace of God teaches us how to live soberly.

- The grace of God teaches us how to live righteously.

- The grace of God teaches us how to live a godly life in this present age.

- The grace of God teaches us how to look for the

blessed hope and glorious appearing of our great God and Savior Jesus Christ.

- The grace of God teaches us how to live a life that is appreciative of the price Rabbi Jesus paid on the cross for our complete redemption.

- The grace of God redeems us from every lawless deed!

- The grace of God purifies us for Jesus' sake so we can be His own special people.

- The grace of God teaches us how to be zealous for good works.

Don't misunderstand why I have come. I did not come to abolish the law of Moses or the writings of the prophets. No, I came to accomplish their purpose (Matthew 5:17 NLT).

A huge theological divide exists in the minds of many believers who declare that Jesus came to abolish the Law of Moses. Yet Rabbi Jesus, in Matthew 5:17, disagrees with this notion. While it is true that New Testament believers are not under the law but under grace, it's a great misunderstanding to believe that the Law of Moses was an enemy of grace. Grace saves us from sin (see Ephesians 2:8) and teaches us how to deny ungodliness, but grace will never reveal your sin to you. Only the law can do that!

> **Grace saves you from sin and teaches how to deny ungodliness, but only the law can reveal your sin to you.**

Justification before God under grace is based purely on believing in the finished work of Jesus Christ on the cross, who alone fulfilled the righteous demands of the law and paid the penalty of sin. However, in the desire for super-spirituality or self-righteousness, I have seen some well-meaning Christians mix the law and grace in terms of achieving justification before God. The apostle Paul calls this witchcraft; and if it's witchcraft, it opens doors for satan to bring accusations against us before the Courts of Heaven. I believe one of the open doors that satan uses to bring accusations against people of destiny is in the area of mixing law and grace in terms of achieving righteousness.

> *But if, while we seek to be justified by Christ, we ourselves also are found sinners, is Christ therefore a minister of sin? Certainly not! For if I build again those things which I destroyed, I make myself a transgressor. For I through the law died to the law that I might live to God* (Galatians 2:17-19 NKJV).

I am so glad that this passage of Scripture in Galatians 2 is in the Bible, written by the same apostle Paul who also wrote Romans 6:14. The apostle Paul poses a very important question here, which is, *"But if, while we seek to be justified by Christ, we ourselves also are found sinners, is Christ therefore a minister of sin?"* The question he poses is very relevant in the current culture of hypergrace. Obviously, people in his day were also misrepresenting grace and using it as a cloak of unrighteousness. Paul felt the need to bring some correction to these people's understanding of grace. "Yes, we are under grace," Paul seemed to be saying, "but this does not give us the license to live in sin or have a certain level of tolerance for it!" Then he followed it up with an equally important statement when he declared, *"For if I build again those things which I destroyed, I make myself a transgressor."* Please let this statement sink in!

> **Living under grace has a much higher standard, morally and spiritually, than living under the Law of Moses.**

Rabbi Jesus gives us a stern warning that we must not forget within the context of defending the Law of Moses and the writing of the prophets. Matthew 5:20 declares, *"But I warn you—unless your righteousness is better than the righteousness of the teachers of religious law and the Pharisees, you will never enter the Kingdom of Heaven!"* In other words, Rabbi Jesus is showing us that living under grace has a much higher standard, morally and spiritually, than living under the Law of Moses.

I have been crucified with Christ; it is no longer I who live, but Christ lives in me; and the life which I now live in the flesh I live by faith in the Son of God, who loved me and gave Himself for me. I do not set aside the grace of God; for if righteousness comes through the law, then Christ died in vain (Galatians 2:20-21 NKJV).

Remember, the root issue between the law and grace is always how righteousness or justification before God is achieved. Any thought of "it's Jesus plus something else" means we are guilty of adding our baggage to His finished work. This negates the true power of God's grace. I am convinced that there are cases in the Courts of Heaven that satan has filed against many believers for frustrating the grace of God through their conceited self-righteousness.

The truth of the matter is that many Christians' compromise, or sin, is due to self-preservation. But the day we lay down our life on the cross of Christ and the altar of total obedience to God, when our life means nothing to us—then satan cannot use the rudimentary elements of this world to scare us into sinning against God. What a powerful place to be! This lifestyle of surrender also gives us spiritual stature in the Courts of Heaven to command the favorable attention of our righteous Judge.

Introspection Questions and Scenarios

Seriously and truthfully examine the list cited from the book of Titus and write why there is something seriously wrong with how current progressive Christian teachers teach grace.

_____

_____

_____

_____

_____

_____

_____

Why would God want to abolish such a powerful instrument as the Law of Moses before the restoration of all things and the end of the age of sin?

_____

_____

_____

_____

_____

_____

_____

Do today's nations need a stable moral compass for a law-abiding and civil society to survive, such as what the Ten Commandments provide?

_____

_____

_____

_____

_____

_____

_____

Some believers misrepresent the grace of God by using it as an excuse to sin, and many are frustrating the grace of God by operating in a spirit of self-righteousness, wanting to add their religious works to God's grace. What is wrong with this mindset?

_____

_____

_____

_____

_____

_____

_____

Scripture Study and Soul Searching

Prayerfully consider each of the following Scriptures relevant in this session and write your thoughts regarding how Rabbi Jesus fulfills the Law of Moses:

Romans 6:14

_____

_____

_____

_____

_____

_____

Titus 2:11-14

_____

_____

_____

_____

_____

_____

_____

Matthew 5:17

_____

_____

_____

_____

_____

_____

_____

Romans 7:18,25

_____

_____

_____

_____

_____

_____

_____

Romans 3:20

_____

_____

_____

_____

_____

_____

_____

Romans 7:14-15

_____

_____

_____

_____

_____

_____

_____

Luke 24:44

_____

_____

_____

_____

_____

_____

_____

Galatians 3:23-24

_____

_____

_____

_____

_____

_____

_____

Ephesians 2:8

_____

_____

_____

_____

_____

_____

_____

Romans 7:12

_____

_____

_____

_____

_____

_____

_____

Matthew 5:18

_____

_____

_____

_____

_____

_____

_____

John 1:17

_____

_____

_____

_____

_____

_____

_____

Romans 4:16

John 1:17

Matthew 5:19

Matthew 5:20

_____

_____

_____

_____

_____

_____

Exodus 20:3-17

_____

_____

_____

_____

_____

_____

Galatians 2:16-19

_____

_____

_____

_____

_____

_____

Galatians 2:20-21

_____
_____
_____
_____
_____
_____
_____

Revelation 12:10-11

_____
_____
_____
_____
_____
_____
_____

Hebrews 12:24

_____
_____
_____
_____
_____
_____
_____

Activation Application

I refuse any teaching on grace that does not lead to the amazing work of the Holy Spirit in the human heart described in Titus 2:11-14. I am convinced that many of the accusations of satan in the Courts of Heaven against believers are due to the sin of transforming the grace of God into licentiousness.

Define "licentiousness." Knowing that definition, would satan find you guilty of the sin of transforming the grace of God into licentiousness? Explain and then take steps to rid that sin from your life.

_____

_____

_____

_____

_____

_____

_____

_____

Define "personal baggage." Because of your personal baggage that you haul around with you, would satan find you guilty of adding your baggage to what Jesus did for you on the cross? Explain how and when you are going to get rid of all destructive baggage.

_____

_____

_____

_____

_____

_____

Reflections and Ruminations

One of the best gifts the Jewish people gave the world was providing a sustainable and duplicatable legal framework for building a just and civil society. This is why Moses is called the lawgiver. Law-abiding nations, almost without exception, are built on the legal framework God gave to Moses.

When the United States started pulling down the Ten Commandments from government buildings, I knew then that the days of the United States remaining a pinnacle nation were numbered, and I also knew that demonization of the nation would increase, and with it a moral decadence never seen before. I was right! Look at the Ten Commandments again and tell me if you would like to live in a country where *"You shall not kill"* or *"You shall not bear false witness"* no longer means anything? So why would Rabbi Jesus abolish the Law of Moses before the nature of sin in the hearts of rebels has been totally vanquished?

Your answer:

_____

_____

_____

_____

_____

_____

_____

_____

_____

_____

_____

_____

_____

_____

_____

_____

Prayers and Proclamations

Your prayers can absolutely usher you into God's presence in the Courts of Heaven. Upon arriving there, allow the Holy Spirit, your Advocate, to guide you into proclaiming Jesus, the One who redeemed you from hell and set you free.

Heavenly Father, even as I stand in Your Royal and Supreme Court, I present myself as a living sacrifice, according to Romans 12:1. Righteous Judge, I petition the Courts of Heaven to judge and remove everything that is blocking intimacy with the Holy Spirit, based on the finished work of Rabbi Jesus on the cross. Father God, I repent for my personal transgressions and for the iniquities of my ancestors that have grieved the Holy Spirit, in Jesus' name I pray. Lord, I repent for every sin of my ancestors that the devil is using as a legal right to stifle my relationship with the Holy Spirit. I also repent for self-inflicted word curses and all covenants with demons that have existed in my ancestral bloodline. I ask, Lord, that every covenant with demonic powers that is keeping me spiritually weak is now revoked and that their legal right to claim me and my bloodline are now dismissed before Your Court, in Jesus' name.

I proclaim and receive and reinforce my relationship with the Holy Spirit that the blood of Rabbi Jesus purchased for me!

I declare and cast down and nullify all of satan's accusations against me!

I proclaim that whatever I bind on earth is what is already bound in Heaven!

I surrender all rights of self-representation in the Courts of Heaven. Instead I ask the Lord Jesus Christ who is my faithful Advocate to plead for me before You!

Session Summary Notes

Jesus: Our Judge and Advocate

My little children, these things I write to you, so that you may not sin. And if anyone sins, we have an Advocate with the Father, Jesus Christ the righteous. And He Himself is the propitiation for our sins, and not for ours only but also for the whole world (1 John 2:1-2 NKJV).

Propitiation" is the act of gaining the favor of or making things right with someone, especially after having done something wrong. Some synonyms are settlement, peace offering, abatement, and so forth, which point to a work that is legal in nature. The passage in 1 John 2 demonstrates the legal nature of Rabbi Jesus' finished work. For this reason, I love referring to Rabbi Jesus' finished work when I am presenting cases for myself or on behalf of others in the Courts of Heaven. Jesus' suffering, death, and resurrection made things right between God and humankind and restored God's favor.

Zechariah 3 is an Old Testament theophany of Rabbi Jesus. Theophanies are essentially the foreshadowing of Messiah in the Old Covenant books of the Bible. Most biblical scholars agree that the Old Testament phrase "the Angel of the Lord" whenever capitalized is a reference to Messiah (the second member of the eternal Godhead). This makes for interesting reading because it shows us that even before His incarnation, Messiah's role in the Courts of Heaven was always one of advocacy on behalf of His people under assault from satan.

In Zechariah 3:1-4, we see an actual heavenly courtroom trial in session. On trial was Joshua, the high priest over the temple in Jerusalem. It's obvious that satan had found some legal grounds to accuse him or prosecute him in the Courts of Heaven. The Bible is very clear that

satan was standing in the Courts of Heaven to oppose the life and ministry of Joshua.

Thankfully, the second member of the eternal Godhead was also in the same courtroom to defend the rights and destiny of the accused high priest. It's obvious that if the Angel of the Lord had not been advocating for Joshua's plight in the Courts of Heaven during this trial, satan would've walked away with a default judgment against Joshua and his priestly ministry would've been severely limited.

The Angel of the Lord advocated for Joshua's plight in the Courts of Heaven.

I'm so thankful that the Lord Jesus Christ is our royal High Priest under the order of Melchizedek and that He also operates as our faithful Advocate in such a powerful and supernatural court.

To the general assembly and church of the firstborn who are registered in heaven, to God the Judge of all, to the spirits of just men made perfect, to Jesus the Mediator of the new covenant, and to the blood of sprinkling that speaks better things than that of Abel (Hebrews 12:23-24 NKJV).

As our heavenly Mediator, the first mediation Rabbi Jesus accomplished was to reconcile God and humankind. We know that from the fall of Adam and Eve in the Garden of Eden there has been a serious spiritual breach between God and humanity. In paying the penalty of our sin and fulfilling the righteous demands of the Law, the Lord Jesus managed to heal the breach between God and humans.

For we must all appear before the judgment seat of Christ, that each one may receive the things done in the body, according to what he has done, whether good or bad (2 Corinthians 5:10 NKJV).

The apostle Paul takes the reality of Jesus as Judge even further in 2 Corinthians 5:10. Paul makes it very clear that each of us will appear before the judgment seat of Christ. According to the apostle, the purpose of the judgment seat of Christ is so we may receive rewards or punishment for things done in the body, whether good or bad. From the study of Scripture we know that the judgment seat of Christ is only for the redeemed. So the judgment seat of Christ is not about eternal damnation. It's about the judgment of our works of faith.

The judgment seat of Christ is about the judgment of our works of faith.

At the judgment seat of Christ, Rabbi Jesus will decide whether what we did on earth was based on right or wrong motives. It is where anything done without the direction of the Holy Spirit will be destroyed. Every act done in the flesh will be destroyed by fire. We will not receive any eternal rewards for anything we did in the flesh. Our spirit will be saved, but as ones who pass through the fire. The judgment seat of Christ is not for unbelievers. Theirs is a different judgment seat, where the unredeemed and unrepentant will appear.

For I know of nothing against myself, yet I am not justified by this; but He who judges me is the Lord. Therefore judge nothing before the time, until the Lord comes, who will both bring to light the hidden things of darkness and reveal the counsels of the hearts. Then each one's praise will come from God (1 Corinthians 4:4-5 NKJV).

Due to the spiritual dynamics of the judgment seat of Christ, in 1 Corinthians 4:4-5 the apostle Paul admonishes us not to be hasty in our judgments. This is because from a human perspective things are not always as they seem. Some people we admire on earth as being ahead of us in matters of destiny may actually be doing things that the Lord never called them to do.

The Judge will "bring to light the hidden things of darkness and reveal the counsels of the hearts."

We will be shocked that some of the ministries who are preaching on television were never called by God to be on television. And some people who were called to a television ministry were so fearful they never ever pursued that dream. We'll find out that some people started churches without the instruction from the Holy Spirit. For this reason, Paul cautions us, *"Therefore judge nothing before the time, until the Lord comes."* Why? Because when Rabbi Jesus takes His seat as Judge, He will *"bring to light the hidden things of darkness and reveal the counsels of the hearts."*

Perhaps there is no human trial more famous in the canon of human history than the trial of Rabbi Jesus by

Pontius Pilate, a Roman governor. This was truly the trial of the century. The million-dollar question is, why would God allow it as part His plan of redemption? I believe in part it was because God could see through the periscope of history and saw the conspiracy of the Sanhedrin council to deny the resurrection of Jesus by bribing the Roman soldiers who were guarding the tomb. Unfortunately for them, the Romans kept meticulous records, especially of high-profile trials that took place under the Roman judicial system. This means that the trial of Jesus cannot be erased from human history.

I also believe God allowed the trial to proceed to fulfill all righteousness before the courts of men and the Courts of Heaven. When Rabbi Jesus stood before Pontius Pilate, He made it clear to the Roman governor that he would have no authority over Him except for the fact that it was given to him from above (God in Heaven).

> ## The trial of Jesus can never be erased from human history.

If the trial of Rabbi Jesus teaches us anything, it is that our adversary has no qualms about taking us before the Courts of Heaven based on true or frivolous accusations. Thankfully, Rabbi Jesus showed up for trial to answer for Himself. Unfortunately, many Christians are suffering unnecessarily because they do not have the revelation of the Courts of Heaven. So when satan brings a railing accusation against them in the Courts of Heaven, they have no ability to respond to the prompting of the Holy Spirit to step into the Courts of Heaven to plead the blood of Jesus against these accusations. Like Job, they end up becoming victims of their lack of knowledge of the operations of the Courts of Heaven in the invisible realm.

Introspection Questions and Scenarios

During this current season or particular point in your spiritual journey, what case(s) is your Advocate presenting on your behalf in the Courts of Heaven?

_____

_____

_____

_____

_____

_____

_____

_____

Has your Advocate had to present this same defense in previous seasons of your life? Is this an issue you need to bring to the Lord with more prayer and fasting? Thoughtfully read Psalm 35:13; Daniel 9:3; Matthew 17:21; Mark 9:29; Luke 2:37; 1 Corinthians 7:5 before writing your answer.

_____

_____

_____

_____

_____

_____

_____

_____

At the judgment seat of Christ, Rabbi Jesus decides whether what we did on earth was based on right or wrong motives. Anything done without the direction of the Holy Spirit and done in the flesh will be destroyed by fire, and we will receive no eternal rewards. Our spirit will be saved, yet as ones who pass through the fire. Thinking back over the past week—does Rabbi Jesus have cause to shout "Hallelujah" at how you went about your days with right motives?

_____

_____

_____

_____

_____

_____

When the Judge brings to light the hidden things of darkness and reveals what is in your heart, will you and the Judge rejoice together? Or will there be a moment of regret? Write what you see happening at that time.

_____

_____

_____

_____

_____

_____

After reading the book and sincerely working through this study guide, how thankful are you knowing that both your Judge and Advocate are on your side—pleased to represent you and rule in your favor as a precious child of Almighty God?

_____

_____

_____

_____

_____

_____

Scripture Study and Soul Searching

Prayerfully consider each of the following Scriptures relevant in this session and write your thoughts regarding Jesus as your Judge and Advocate:

1 John 2:1-2

_____

_____

_____

_____

_____

_____

Zechariah 3:1-4

_____

_____

_____

_____

_____

_____

Hebrews 12:23-24

_____

_____

_____

_____

_____

_____

Acts 17:28-31

_____

_____

_____

_____

_____

_____

_____

2 Corinthians 5:10

_____

_____

_____

_____

_____

_____

_____

1 Corinthians 4:4-5

_____

_____

_____

_____

_____

_____

_____

Revelation 20:11-15

_____

_____

_____

_____

_____

_____

_____

Luke 23:1-4

_____

_____

_____

_____

_____

_____

_____

John 18:33

_____

_____

_____

_____

_____

_____

_____

John 18:29-30

_____

_____

_____

_____

_____

_____

_____

Matthew 26:65

_____

_____

_____

_____

_____

_____

_____

Mark 14:63-64

_____

_____

_____

_____

_____

_____

_____

Matthew 26:52

_____

_____

_____

_____

_____

_____

John 18:36

_____

_____

_____

_____

_____

_____

_____

John 18:38

_____

_____

_____

_____

_____

_____

_____

John 18:29-30

_____

_____

_____

_____

_____

_____

_____

John 18:15

_____

_____

_____

_____

_____

_____

_____

Matthew 12:24

_____

_____

_____

_____

_____

_____

Acts 4:13-18

_____

_____

_____

_____

_____

_____

_____

Job 1:6-12

_____

_____

_____

_____

_____

_____

_____

_____

John 11:43-44

_____

_____

_____

_____

_____

_____

_____

John 11:53

John 11:57

John 12:10-11

Activation Application

For we must all stand before Christ to be judged. We will each receive whatever we deserve for the good or evil we have done in this earthly body (2 Corinthians 5:10 NLT).

Research in God's Word, the Bible, His various judgments and relationships with those on the following list, all the while reflecting on the circumstances of each and the resulting action.

The judgment of:

	Relevant Scripture(s)	Outcome
Adam and Eve		
Assyria		
Babylon		
Centurion		
Demons		
Egypt		
Esther		
Golden calf makers		
Humans (time of Noah)		
Isaac		
Israelites		
Jacob		
Jezebel		
Job		
Jonah		

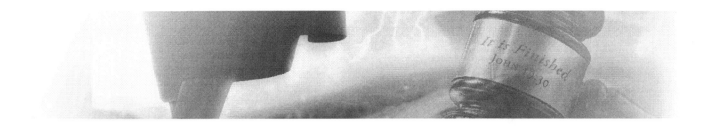

	Relevant Scripture(s)	Outcome
Judas		
King David		
Lot's wife		
Lucifer		
Mary (Jesus' mother)		
Moses		
Pharaoh		
Pilate		
Samson		
Sanhedrin		
Sapphira and Ananias		
Satan		
Serpent		
Sodom and Gomorrah		
Tower of Babel builders		
Zacchaeus		
Others:		
The future you:		

Prayers and Proclamation

Your prayers can absolutely usher you into God's presence in the Courts of Heaven. Upon arriving there, allow the Holy Spirit, your Advocate, to guide you into proclaiming Jesus, the One who redeemed you from hell and set you free.

My Father in Heaven, thank You for placing Rabbi Jesus at the center of Your divine symphony of advocacy in the Courts of Heaven on my behalf against satan's accusation and encroachments. I know I am admonished not to sin, but if I do, the Holy Spirit passionately reminds me that we have an Advocate with You the righteous Judge. I am so very grateful, Lord, that Your most capable Mediator is pleading my plight in the Courts of Heaven; if not, satan could walk away with a default judgment against me, and reaching my full God-given potential would be severely limited. As the blood of Abel cries for vengeance and vindication, the blood of Rabbi Jesus cries for redemption, restoration, and forgiveness— for me. I realize that I have a very powerful voice speaking on my behalf in the Courts of Heaven because His blood's testimony is steady and sure. All glory and honor to You! Amen, in Jesus' cherished name.

I proclaim that Rabbi Jesus will successfully declare victory for me in the Courts of Heaven!

I declare that the blood of Jesus assures my acquittal before the Judge of the universe!

I proclaim that the knowledge I have been given about the Courts of Heaven prepares me to stand strong and confident against my accuser!

I declare that any true or frivolous charges against me will be dismissed by my holy Judge!

Session Summary Notes

Legal Ramifications of the Cross

For the message of the cross is foolishness [absurd and illogical] to those who are perishing and spiritually dead [because they reject it], but to us who are being saved [by God's grace] it is [the manifestation of] the power of God (1 Corinthians 1:18 AMP).

The cross of Christ gives veracity to the importance and the reality of the Courts of Heaven. The cross is the actual justification for the seriousness of sin and the importance of the Law of God. No human court would have demanded a death sentence to atone for the sins of the whole world. Rabbi Jesus was crucified on the cross to satisfy the righteous demands of the Law, which says that *"The person who sins is the one who will die"* (Ezekiel 18:20 NLT). What court does the Law of Moses fall under? Obviously the Courts of Heaven, for no earthly court rises to that standard of morality.

In 1 Corinthians 1:18, the apostle Paul clearly states that the message of the cross is foolishness to people who are perishing, but for those of us who are being saved, it's truly a demonstration of the power of God. It is important to focus on the legal ramifications of the cross of Christ and how we can use it as a tool of vindication when presenting our cases in the Courts of Heaven against the adversary.

If a man has committed a sin deserving of death, and he is put to death, and you hang him on a tree, his body shall not remain overnight on the tree, but you shall surely bury him that day, so that you do not defile the land which the Lord your God is giving you
as an inheritance; for he who is hanged is accursed of God (Deuteronomy 21:22-23 NKJV).

How can anyone who is biblically astute not recognize the footprints of Jesus all over this Scripture from Deuteronomy 21 in the Old Testament? Even though Rabbi Jesus never sinned, He nevertheless took our place. Rabbi Jesus became a Man of sin (see 1 Corinthians 15:21). According to the Law of Moses as prescribed in Deuteronomy 21, such a man was found to be deserving of death.

Even though Rabbi Jesus never sinned, He nevertheless became a Man of sin to redeem us.

Many Christians, including most pastors, fail to discern the difference between the law of sin and death and the Law that Rabbi Jesus referenced in Matthew 5:17: *"Don't misunderstand why I have come. I did not come to abolish the law of Moses or the writings of the prophets. No, I came to accomplish their purpose."* We cannot fully appreciate the legal ramification of the cross without making clear this distinction.

Paul does indeed say that the law of the Spirit of life in Christ Jesus has set us free from the law of sin and death. Nevertheless, does this release us from obedience to God's Ten Commandment law? Are God's Ten Commandments the law of sin and death? Paul answers this mystery:

Well then, am I suggesting that the law of God is sinful? Of course not! In fact, it was the law that showed me my sin. I would never have known that coveting is wrong if the law had not said, "You must not covet" (Romans 7:7 NLT).

Are we freed from the law of sin and death that reigns in our members, or are we released from obeying the just and holy law of God? Obviously, we are freed from the law of sin and death—but not from obeying the holy and just law of God.

Even under our beautiful dispensation of grace, *"Thou shall not kill"* still applies to us. We must understand the wisdom of Rabbi Jesus—in not abolishing the Law of Moses, He fulfilled the aspects of the Law of Moses we could never satisfy. This why satan is having fun dragging God's children into the Courts of Heaven, accusing us of being lawbreakers—too many have fallen for the hyper-grace mantra.

The cross is central to understanding righteousness by faith—it does not stand in opposition to the righteous and moral law of God. If the law of Moses could be changed or set aside, or if sin could be ignored, then Jesus would not have needed to die! There would have been no need for the cross. While we cannot achieve righteousness by keeping the law, we must nevertheless maintain the disposition of abiding in Christ and being led by the Holy Spirit to escape the righteous demands of the law under the New Testament (see Romans 8:14). For those who are led by the Holy Spirit and walk in love, there is no law—the Holy Spirit will never lead you to violate divine morality.

On the cross Rabbi Jesus disarmed principalities and powers—the supernatural forces of evil that were operating against us. Rabbi Jesus made a public example of these demonic entities in His triumphal procession after having triumphed over them through the cross. When you invoke the finished work of Rabbi Jesus on the cross against the accusations and tactics of the adversary, satan, you will win every time. Hallelujah!

Introspection Questions and Scenarios

"The message of the cross is foolish to those who are headed for destruction! But we who are being saved know it is the very power of God" (1 Corinthians 1:18 NLT). As someone who is *"being saved,"* how do you define the *"message of the cross"*?

_____

_____

_____

_____

_____

_____

_____

How could Moses write in the Old Testament what happened centuries later in the New Testament, before Jesus was even born, lived, and then died on the cross?

_____

_____

_____

_____

_____

_____

_____

The cross is central to understanding righteousness by faith, and it does not stand in opposition to the righteous and moral law of God. If the law of Moses could be changed or set aside, or if sin could be ignored, Jesus would not have needed to die—no need for the cross! Explain this realization and truth in your own words.

_____

_____

_____

_____

_____

_____

_____

There is no law for those who are led by the Holy Spirit and walk in love, because the Holy Spirit will never lead us into violating divine morality. Why is it so vital for believers, for you, to be led through life by the Holy Spirit?

_____

_____

_____

_____

_____

_____

_____

The cross and Rabbi Jesus' sacrificial death at Calvary are all about a broken law. A broken law, or sin, results in death, according to Romans 6:23. Satan hates that righteous, good, and just law. He will do everything in his power to wage war against it with all the cunning he can muster.

*When you were dead in your sins and in the uncircumcision of your flesh (worldliness, manner of life), God made you alive together with Christ, having [freely] forgiven us all our sins, having **canceled out the certificate of debt consisting of legal demands** [which were in force] against us and which were hostile to us. And this certificate He has set aside and completely removed by **nailing it to the cross**. When He had disarmed the rulers and authorities [those supernatural forces of evil operating against us], He made a public example of them [exhibiting them as captives in His triumphal procession], having triumphed over them through the cross* (Colossians 2:13-15 AMP).

Rabbi Jesus canceled the certificate of debt, set it aside, and completely removed it as well as disarmed principalities, powers, and supernatural forces of evil operating against us and nailed it all to the cross. What is your responsibility to acknowledge all that Jesus did for you and the whole of humanity by His sacrifice?

_____

_____

_____

_____

_____

_____

_____

_____

Do you believe that when you invoke the truth of the finished work of Rabbi Jesus on the cross against the accusations and tactics of the adversary in the Courts of Heaven you will win every time?

_____

_____

_____

_____

_____

_____

_____

_____

Scripture Study and Soul Searching

Prayerfully consider each of the following Scriptures relevant in this session and write your thoughts regarding the legal ramifications of the cross:

1 Corinthians 1:18

_____

_____

_____

_____

_____

_____

_____

Ezekiel 18:20

_____

_____

_____

_____

_____

_____

_____

Galatians 3:10

_____

_____

_____

_____

_____

_____

_____

Galatians 3:13-14

_____
_____
_____
_____
_____
_____
_____

Deuteronomy 21:22-23

_____
_____
_____
_____
_____
_____
_____

John 19:40-42

_____
_____
_____
_____
_____
_____
_____

Romans 8:1-2

_____

_____

_____

_____

_____

_____

Romans 7:7

_____

_____

_____

_____

_____

_____

_____

Romans 7:13-14

_____

_____

_____

_____

_____

_____

_____

Romans 7:21-25

_____

_____

_____

_____

_____

_____

_____

John 19:29-30

_____

_____

_____

_____

_____

_____

_____

Galatians 2:20

_____

_____

_____

_____

_____

_____

_____

Colossians 2:13-15

_____

_____

_____

_____

_____

_____

_____

Activation Application

Many Christians, including most pastors, fail to discern the difference between the law of sin and death and the Law that Rabbi Jesus referenced in Matthew 5:17: *"Don't misunderstand why I have come. I did not come to abolish the law of Moses or the writings of the prophets. No, I came to accomplish their purpose."* After reading this chapter in the book and completing this session of the study guide, do you now fully appreciate the legal ramification of the cross, and is this distinction clear? Write yes or no and your reasoning:

_____

_____

_____

_____

_____

_____

_____

_____

_____

Write everything that comes to your attention when you think of the details included on your "certificate of debt"—then thank God that all were forgiven when Rabbi Jesus nailed that certificate to His cross.

_____

_____

_____

_____

_____

_____

_____

_____

_____

Reflections and Ruminations

Reflect on the following odd laws that are still "on the books" in numerous US states. All are active laws but are not necessarily enforced. Then ruminate upon the differences between the biblical Mosaic Law, the Law and the Prophets, and God's ultimate, overarching Law, the Ten Commandments.

Arkansas: You Can't Walk Your Cow After 1 p.m. on Sunday. In Little Rock, it is unlawful to walk one's cow down Main Street after 1 p.m. on a Sunday. So, if you enjoy a Sunday stroll with your bovine bestie, you may have to reconsider Little Rock for your weekend getaway. Furthermore, no livestock of any kind can wear a bell within the city limits after 9 p.m.

California: Women May Not Drive in a Housecoat. Forgot something at the store and need to run out real quick in your bathrobe? That'll be a hard stop if you're a woman in the state of California. This anti-quated (read: bizarre) law prohibits women from operating a motor vehicle while wearing a housecoat. If violated, a woman can be subject to some hefty fines.

Connecticut: A Pickle Must Bounce in Order to Be Sold. If it doesn't bounce, then it's not a pickle, and you can't sell it as one. At least not in the state of Connecticut. The series of statutes come from when a farmer was caught selling pickles that were not fit for human consumption. The man was fined $500 for his imposter pickle business.

Oregon: No Astrologers Allowed. To clarify, this is not a state-wide law. But it is very much a law in the town of Yamhill. Astrology is considered to be a form of the "occult arts," which are illegal to practice in Yamhill. So, if you're looking to know more about your future, definitely don't visit this Oregon town. Also forbidden here are mesmerism, spiritualism, fortune-telling, and palmistry.

Utah: Don't Launch Missiles at Buses. It may seem pretty obvious, but in Utah, they decided to spell it out. It is illegal in the state of Utah (and we hope everywhere else in the country) to hurl a missile at a bus or a bus terminal. If you are a "peace officer" or security personnel, you are exempt from the law, provided you have a pretty good reason to do so.

Wisconsin: All Cheese Must Be Delicious. Wisconsin is certainly the dairy counter of America, known for producing some of the best cheese in the country. You can blame the well-fed cows, the rolling pastures, or maybe even the cheese-making techniques for such delicious cheese, but you may also be interested to know that it is actually the law for Wisconsin cheese to be delicious or, as the legal jargon puts it, "highly delicious." According to the law, "Cheese shall be fine, highly pleasing and free from undesirable flavors and odors."[1]

Note

1. Meagan Drillinger, "These Weird Laws in Every State Are Stranger Than Fiction," *Far&Wide,* January 19, 2022; https://www.farandwide.com/s/weird-laws-every-state-b53030c4911d4929; accessed March 9, 2023.

Prayers and Proclamations

Your prayers can absolutely usher you into God's presence in the Courts of Heaven. Upon arriving there, allow the Holy Spirit, your Advocate, to guide you into proclaiming Jesus, the One who redeemed you from hell and set you free.

Lord God, I come before You with praise and worship for all You have done for me in the Courts of Heaven. No longer do I fret about not being heard in Your courtroom. No longer do I panic about being Your child in need of understanding and compassion and forgiveness. Now I know for certain that Jesus is my Advocate and that He completely wiped away my sins. Thank You for providing Your beloved Son as a Mediator between You and me. Only when I see You face to face will I have the perfect words and ways to show You my unending love and devotion. Until then, please accept my humble and sincere gratitude for the mercy and grace shown me daily, even moment by moment. In Jesus' name, amen.

I proclaim victory over every accusation by the enemy—because of the finished work of Rabbi Jesus on the cross!

I declare that Rabbi Jesus disarmed principalities and powers and supernatural forces of evil that were operating against me!

I proclaim that Rabbi Jesus' sacrificial death at Calvary repaired every broken law!

I declare that I am led by the Holy Spirit and walk in His love and divine morality!

Session Summary Notes

Jesus, the Holy Spirit, and the Courts of Heaven

Nevertheless I tell you the truth. It is to your advantage that I go away; for if I do not go away, the Helper [Holy Spirit] will not come to you; but if I depart, I will send Him to you. And when He has come, He will convict the world of sin, and of righteousness, and of judgment: of sin, because they do not believe in Me; of righteousness, because I go to My Father and you see Me no more; of judgment, because the ruler of this world is judged (John 16:7-11 NKJV).

Rabbi Jesus—who raised the dead, cleansed lepers, opened blind eyes, and cast out demons like no Man before Him—says that it is to our advantage that He goes away because if He doesn't get out of the way, the Holy Spirit will not come. Rabbi Jesus calls the Holy Spirit *"the Helper,"* which translates from the Hebrew language as "legal aid." In addition to leading us in righteousness day by day, one of the other assignments of the Holy Spirit is to be our legal aid in the Courts of Heaven. Why? There is no personality on earth who understands the inner workings and the dynamics of the Courts in Heaven more than the Holy Spirit.

> **The presence of the Holy Spirit on earth globalized the presence of Jesus Christ in all the believing saints all around the world.**

The Holy Spirit comes from the heavenly Kingdom where the Courts are located. So how can we fail to get our petitions heard and granted by the righteous Judge if we are stepping into the Courts of Heaven by the leading of the Holy Spirit? There is no way we can fail.

The first advantage of having the Holy Spirit released on earth versus having the physical Jesus is that the Holy Spirit can indwell millions of people at the same time, while working tirelessly to manifest the character of Jesus in all of them. Such is the power and beauty of having the Holy Spirit. The presence of the Holy Spirit on earth globalized the presence of Jesus Christ in all the believing saints all around the world.

And when he comes, he will convict the world of its sin, and of God's righteousness, and of the coming judgment. The world's sin is that it refuses to believe in me. Righteousness is available because I go to the Father, and you will see me no more. Judgment will come because the ruler of this world has already been judged (John 16:8-11 NLT).

Rabbi Jesus defines the judicial work of the Holy Spirit in three essential aspects: (1) Convict the world of sin; (2) Convict the saints of their imputed righteousness in Christ Jesus; (3) Enforce the judgment of sin and the devil. (My book *Following the Footsteps of Rabbi Jesus into the Courts of Heaven* digs deeper into these three aspects.)

When Rabbi Jesus says the Holy Spirit will convict the word of sin, He is not implying that the Holy Spirit will accuse us of being sinful men and women. No. Satan is the accuser. Jesus "convicts" in the sense that He shows us the true nature of sin and the condition of our hearts before God while pointing the way to salvation. When the devil accuses us, the ultimate goal is to bring us under a spirit of condemnation as well as arrest our spiritual development.

The Holy Spirit convicts us of our righteousness so we can stand before God's righteous throne and boldly proclaim what is rightfully ours according to the inheritance God has given us in Christ Jesus.

The Holy Spirit enforces the judgment of sin and the devil in both the natural and heavenly realms. The Holy Spirit is responsible for making sure God's children know that satan and sin—which gives him the legal grounds to operate in our lives—have both been severely judged in the body of Jesus Christ on the cross. This is the powerful testimony the Holy Spirit gives us each time we step into the Courts of Heaven to claim what is legally ours through the finished work of Jesus on the cross.

It's impossible for satan to lie to us when we're totally yielded to the Holy Spirit.

When the Spirit of truth comes, he will guide you into all truth. He will not speak on his own but will tell you what he has heard. He will tell you about the future. He will bring me glory by telling you whatever he receives from me (John 16:13-14 NLT).

Based on John 16:13-14, Rabbi Jesus finally informs us who the Holy Spirit is and why we desperately need Him. First, Rabbi Jesus tells us that the Holy Spirit is the Spirit of truth. This means that wherever the truth is, your legal aid will find it. Therefore, it's impossible for satan to lie to us when we're totally yielded to the Holy Spirit. Rabbi Jesus also tells us that the Holy Spirit will guide us into *"all truth,"* which means there are some truths about God's Kingdom and our adversary that we don't yet know but will be revealed as we continue to grow spiritually.

The Holy Spirit never contradicts Jesus.

In John 8:2-11, Rabbi Jesus and the Holy Spirit work together to rescue a woman caught in adultery from a horrible death. There are several times in Scripture when the Courts of Heaven have actually descended on earth to render a righteous verdict against or on behalf of someone. In this story, Rabbi Jesus' role is of a righteous Judge over the woman's trial.

However, it's quite clear the Holy Spirit was working behind the scenes to convict the woman's accusers of their own unconfessed sin. One by one they walked away totally convicted of their sin and lawbreaking by the Holy Spirit. This passage of Scripture reveals how Rabbi Jesus and the Holy Spirit operate together in the Courts of Heaven. Remember that you will be working with the triune Godhead as you present cases in the Courts of Heaven.

Introspection Questions and Scenarios

After reading in the book the detailed descriptions of the three essential aspects of the Holy Spirit's judicial role in the Courts of Heaven, write your own definitions here:

_____

_____

_____

_____

_____

_____

_____

As asked in the book, "If your life depended on it and you are in a court of law where you are being falsely accused, wouldn't you do everything humanly possible to secure a legal aid who is also the Spirit of truth?" Answer here:

_____

_____

_____

_____

_____

_____

_____

_____

Christ leaves it up to the Holy Spirit to reveal to us higher realms of truth that unlock the Kingdom of God the deeper and deeper we dive into God. Rabbi Jesus tells us that the Holy Spirit speaks on *"His own authority,"* which means the Holy Spirit never contradicts Jesus. And the Holy Spirit can also give us prophetic insights of the future. If the Holy Spirit ever offered to show you the future, what would you ask Him to see, and why?

_____

_____

_____

_____

_____

_____

_____

How important is it for you to continue to grow spiritually, realizing there are some truths about God's Kingdom and your adversary that have yet to be revealed? Does what you don't know bring angst or excitement? Explain.

_____

_____

_____

_____

_____

_____

_____

Scripture Study and Soul Searching

Prayerfully consider each of the following Scriptures relevant in this session and write your thoughts regarding Jesus, the Holy Spirit, and the Courts of Heaven:

John 16:7-14

_____

_____

_____

_____

_____

Psalm 51:11

_____

_____

_____

_____

_____

_____

Isaiah 63:10-11

_____

_____

_____

_____

_____

_____

Mark 11:17

_____
_____
_____
_____
_____
_____

Luke 3:22

_____
_____
_____
_____
_____
_____

Luke 11:13

_____
_____
_____
_____
_____
_____

John 8:2-11

_____
_____
_____
_____
_____
_____

Activation Application

The definition of "Helper" or *Parakletos* is:

- Summoned, called to one's side, especially called to one's legal aid;
- One who pleads another's cause before a judge, a pleader, counsel for defense, legal assistant, an advocate;
- One who pleads another's cause with one, an intercessor, like Christ in His exaltation at God's right hand, pleading with God the Father for the pardon of our sins;
- In the widest sense, a helper, succourer, aider, assistant. Like the Holy Spirit destined to take the place of Christ with the apostles (after His ascension to the Father) to lead them to a deeper knowledge of the gospel truth and give them divine strength needed to enable them to undergo trials and persecutions on behalf of the divine kingdom.

Of these definitions, which most closely describes your opinion, perspective, or belief about the Holy Spirit?

_____

_____

_____

_____

_____

_____

_____

In what ways has the Holy Spirit been part of your life currently, in the past, and when you look to the future?

_____

_____

_____

_____

_____

_____

_____

Reflections and Ruminations

Reflecting on the following Scripture passage from the Amplified Bible, how important is the Holy Spirit in your life? Why is this Third Person of the Trinity so very crucial in the body of Christ and in particular your life?

But I tell you the truth, it is to your advantage that I go away; for if I do not go away, the Helper (Comforter, Advocate, Intercessor—Counselor, Strengthener, Standby) will not come to you; but if I go, I will send Him (the Holy Spirit) to you [to be in close fellowship with you]. And He, when He comes, will convict the world about [the guilt of] sin [and the need for a Savior], and about righteousness, and about judgment: about sin [and the true nature of it], because they do not believe in Me [and My message]; about righteousness [personal integrity and godly character], because I am going to My Father and you will no longer see Me; about judgment [the certainty of it], because the ruler of this world (Satan) has been judged and condemned (John 16:7-11 AMP).

_____

_____

_____

_____

_____

_____

_____

_____

_____

_____

_____

_____

_____

_____

_____

Prayers and Proclamations

Your prayers can absolutely usher you into God's presence in the Courts of Heaven. Upon arriving there, allow the Holy Spirit, your Advocate, to guide you into proclaiming Jesus, the One who redeemed you from hell and set you free.

Holy Trinity, Your Three-in-One existence is proof positive that to my finite mind, Your love for Your creation is unfathomable. Each Person is intricately moving and living and loving within and throughout all of creation. How blessed am I to be part of that eternal camaraderie and holy partnership! Because the Holy Spirit comes from the heavenly Kingdom where the Courts are located, He is the perfect Advocate to process all my petitions to be heard and granted by the righteous Judge. When I step into the Courts of Heaven by the leading of the Holy Spirit, there is no way the charges of the enemy against me will harm me. Thank You for the power of the Holy Spirit, who is like having Jesus in His humanity on steroids worldwide! May I always honor each Person of the Trinity for the beauty of the Trio who deserve all my praise and worship, now and for eternity. In the precious name of Jesus, amen.

I proclaim the Holy Spirit's triumph in the Courts of Heaven and the devil's defeat!

I declare my right to stand boldly in God's courtroom, claiming what is legally mine according to my inheritance as His child!

I proclaim the finished work of Jesus on the cross that sets every captive free!

I declare that the Holy Spirit will guide me into all truth, for which I give God all the glory in Jesus' name!

Session Summary Notes

Jesus' Legal Work as Our High Priest

Seeing then that we have a great High Priest who has passed through the heavens, Jesus the Son of God, let us hold fast our confession. For we do not have a High Priest who cannot sympathize with our weaknesses, but was in all points tempted as we are, yet without sin. Let us therefore come boldly to the throne of grace, that we may obtain mercy and find grace to help in time of need (Hebrews 4:14-16 NKJV).

Two of the most important roles of Rabbi Jesus after His resurrection and ascension are His work as our merciful High Priest and our faithful Advocate in the Courts of Heaven. It is important to remember that the work of a high priest is very much judicial in nature; as High Priest, He passes through the Courts of Heaven.

One of the assignments of a high priest was to ascertain what kind of sacrifice was required to atone for sin. Rabbi Jesus concluded that only the sacrifice of His own life would atone for our sin. The fact that Rabbi Jesus was willing to die on the cross in our place makes Him our most sufficient Savior indeed. This fact also makes Him one of the most important allies we could ever have in the Courts of Heaven as our loyal Advocate. The writer of the book of Hebrews makes it abundantly clear that Rabbi Jesus is the Priest of a higher priestly order, that of Melchizedek, which is far superior to the Levitical priesthood that the Jewish people were used to.

In the world's judicial systems, there are various categories of courts—civil, criminal, and family courts; in the United States, there is also the Supreme Court. Everything on earth is fashioned after the governmental pattern of Heaven. Like on earth, the spiritual realm has various courts of law. One is the Ancient of Days court, and another is the grace court. Hebrews 4:16 declares, *"Let us therefore come boldly to the throne of grace, that we may obtain mercy and find grace to help in time of need."*

> **Rabbi Jesus concluded that only the sacrifice of His own life would atone for our sin.**

The grace court is an important courtroom in Heaven when it comes to defeating idols and evil altars. Why? The number-one accusation satan brings against you in the Courts of Heaven is when you break God's laws. The Lord's first few commandments are:

You shall have no other gods before Me. You shall not make for yourself a carved image—any likeness of anything that is in heaven above, or that is in the earth beneath, or that is in the water under the earth; you shall not bow down to them nor serve them (Exodus 20:2-5 NKJV).

Idolatry is breaking God's laws. Fortunately, through the power of His grace, the Lord has made it possible for you to overcome all of the devil's indictments. The apostle Paul explains how:

I do not ignore or nullify the [gracious gift of the] grace of God [His amazing, unmerited favor], for if righteousness comes through [observing] the Law, then Christ died needlessly. [His suffering and death would have had no purpose whatsoever] (Galatians 2:21 AMP).

The Bible says it's impossible to keep the whole law (see James 2:10). That's why Jesus, the only sinless Person in the history of the earth, fulfilled the righteous requirements of the law for you and me on the cross (see Romans 8:4). Grace is the power that imparts this truth so we can be justified, made righteous, and acquitted of every charge the enemy brings against our lawbreaking.

Grace imparts Christ's righteousness to us.

That's why you must never ignore, set aside, invalidate, frustrate, or nullify God's grace in your life. You need grace because it imparts Christ's righteousness to you. If you think you can walk perfectly before God without breaking His commandments, you are mistaken. Believing so says that you didn't need Jesus to die for you and that He was crucified in vain. (See our book *Idols Riot: Prosecuting Idols and Evil Altars from the Courts of Heaven* by Francis Myles and Katie Souza.)

*This **hope** [this confident assurance] we have as **an anchor of the soul** [it cannot slip and it cannot break down under whatever pressure bears upon it]—**a safe and steadfast hope that enters within the veil** [of the heavenly temple, that most Holy Place in which the very presence of God dwells], where Jesus*

has entered [in advance] as a forerunner for us, having become a High Priest forever according to the order of Melchizedek (Hebrews 6:19-20 AMP).

Hebrews 6:19-20 makes it clear that Rabbi Jesus has entered in advance as a *"forerunner"* for all of us behind the veil. What is behind the veil? The most Holy Place where the presence of God dwells and abides. Rabbi Jesus has secured in the Kingdom of Heaven a hope that is an *"anchor of the soul."* Our soul consists of our will, mind, and emotions—the true seat of self. This means we can access all the secrets of God's presence in real time!

Since none of us are righteous, nor can we deliver ourselves through our own efforts, our imputed righteousness in Christ Jesus becomes a powerful inflection point for diffusing all the accusations of the enemy against us. However, this is not the only scale of justice that the Lord uses to make sure that we are still in the faith and are following the leading of the Holy Spirit.

Never ignore, set aside, invalidate, frustrate, or nullify God's grace in your life.

Peace is one of the critical scales of justice that the Holy Spirit uses to determine whether we have confidence toward God or whether our own heart is condemning us. If there are areas in our lives we have not brought under subjection to the lordship of Jesus Christ, we won't have peace. It's difficult to present our case boldly and faithfully against satan in the Courts of Heaven when our heart is condemning us. Lack of peace in our soul is always a good indicator that something is wrong spiritually.

As a rule, I remain prayerful when I'm restless until the Lord shows me why I don't have peace. Lack of peace may point to the very thing satan is using to level accusations against me and giving him legal grounds against me in the Courts of Heaven.

Introspection Questions and Scenarios

Because your soul consists of your will, mind, and emotions—the true seat of self—on a scale from 1 (least) to 10 (most), rank who has the most control over each part of your soul, you or your heavenly Father. Think a few moments before ranking and writing your reasoning:

	You	God
Your will	_____	_____

_____

_____

_____

| **Your mind** | _____ | _____ |

_____

_____

_____

| **Your emotions** | _____ | _____ |

_____

_____

_____

What can you do to increase the ranking so that your soul is totally controlled by God and your rating is 10 for will, mind, and emotions? Do you believe this is even possible?

_____

_____

_____

_____

_____

_____

_____

Of the Ten Commandments (see Exodus 20:1-17 and Matthew 22:36-39), which two are the hardest to keep? Which two are the easiest? Why?

_____

_____

_____

_____

_____

_____

_____

Thinking of the word and concept of "peace," write what first comes to mind, then write what it means from your heart, then write how it affects your emotions. What is the difference between these definitions and the peace of God that passes all understanding? (See Philippians 4:7.)

_____

_____

_____

_____

_____

_____

_____

When you're restless or feel agitated, what may this mean for the enemy who goes before the Courts of Heaven with evil intent? How do you find peace during times of stress or seemingly overwhelming circumstances?

_____

_____

_____

_____

_____

_____

_____

Scripture Study and Soul Searching

Prayerfully consider each of the following Scriptures relevant in this session and write your thoughts regarding Jesus' legal work as your High Priest:

Hebrews 5:1-6

_____

_____

_____

_____

_____

Hebrews 2:14-18

_____

_____

_____

_____

_____

Hebrews 4:14-16

_____

_____

_____

_____

_____

Galatians 2:21

_____

_____

_____

_____

_____

Hebrews 6:19-20

_____

_____

_____

_____

_____

Hebrews 7:1-2

_____

_____

_____

_____

_____

Hebrews 2:17-18

_____

_____

_____

_____

_____

Activation Application

List some of the ways Rabbi Jesus in His human form suffered while on earth. Then list the ways you have suffered for the cause of Christ. Is it reasonable to presume that you can resist and overcome the same temptations and sufferings as the Savior? Write your reasonings.

_____

_____

_____

_____

_____

_____

_____

_____

_____

_____

_____

In the context of Jesus and His legal work as our High Priest, write a scenario that describes you and your High Priest entering the Courts of Heaven, the proceedings, the verdict, and the celebration.

_____

_____

_____

_____

_____

_____

_____

_____

_____

Reflections and Ruminations

After reading this summarized excerpt from the book *Following the Footsteps of Rabbi Jesus into the Courts of Heaven,* reflect on the magnitude and significance of what Rabbi Jesus did for all of humanity and for you.

The writer of Hebrews says that Rabbi Jesus became like humans in all things and in all points. God was setting Him up to be an empathetic and merciful High Priest; therefore, He's not a stranger to human temptation and frailty. God could now feel hungry in Christ Jesus. God could get tired in the body of Jesus. God could get physically attacked in the body of Jesus. For Messiah in His divinity before the immaculate conception, these human constructs did not apply to Him.

As a human, Rabbi Jesus, though He was God incarnate, experienced suffering in His human body. He suffered the constant abuse of the Pharisees and Sadducees. He suffered the human idiosyncrasies of His own disciples. He was also tempted in every way. Rabbi Jesus had to be tempted in every way and yet He did not sin. Wow! What a Man to have defending us—our royal Advocate in the Courts of Heaven.

Although the High Priest on earth, He gave up His majesty in Heaven for us, for you. Ruminate on the incomprehensible "downgrade" Jesus experienced.

_____

_____

_____

_____

_____

_____

_____

_____

_____

_____

_____

_____

_____

_____

_____

_____

_____

Prayers and Proclamations

Your prayers can absolutely usher you into God's presence in the Courts of Heaven. Upon arriving there, allow the Holy Spirit, your Advocate, to guide you into proclaiming Jesus, the One who redeemed you from hell and set you free.

My Lord and Savior, Your role as my High Priest in the Courts of Heaven is more than I could ask or imagine—or deserve. No other god would make the sacrifice You have for me. I am so very thankful for Your empathetic and compassionate love for me. With the help of the Holy Spirit I pray that my lawbreaking days have ended and that the enemy will have no cause to accuse me in Your courts. I pray, Lord, that I will never ignore, set aside, invalidate, frustrate, or nullify God's grace in my life. I need Your grace because it imparts Christ's righteousness to me. My first line of defense when standing in the Courts of Heaven is my position of righteousness in Christ Jesus. Father God, I know I am not righteous on my own, nor can I deliver myself through my own efforts; rather, my imputed righteousness in Christ Jesus becomes a powerful inflection point for diffusing all the accusations of the enemy against me. Your peace that passes all my understanding is the proof of Your divine alignment in my life. Thank You! In Jesus' name, amen.

I proclaim that Rabbi Jesus is the Priest of the highest priestly order!

I declare that High Priest Jesus is merciful and faithful in all things pertaining to God!

I proclaim that Rabbi Jesus gave me the right to resist the spirit of death!

I declare that the devil has no legal grounds against me in the Courts of Heaven!

Session Summary Notes

The Blood of Jesus and the Courts of Heaven

*For **the life of the flesh is in the blood**, and I have given it to you on the altar to make atonement for your souls; for **it is the blood that makes atonement**, by reason of the life [which it represents]* (Leviticus 17:11 AMP).

The Bible is very clear about how valuable blood is. All *"life of the flesh"* (you and I included) is in the blood. The life of all flesh (animals included) is not in the brain, it's not in the kidneys—it is in the blood; making blood the most precious commodity for sustaining life that God created.

Because life of all flesh is in the blood, God decided to give it to us on the altar to make atonement for our sinful soul. In Leviticus 17:11, Moses states clearly that blood makes atonement, which literally means "to make one with God." Blood can be used as payment for human souls because it represents life.

All people have sinned and fallen short of the glory of God. But...

Nevertheless, all humans are descendants of the first Adam and have sinned and fallen short of the glory of God (see Romans 3:23). That means that all blood is compromised by the law of sin and death. When Adam and Eve sinned, they opened the door for sin, iniquity, and transgression to enter the human genome. This is why no human being on earth had blood God could have used to atone for our sinful souls—and why God waited more than 4,000 years until the miraculous conception of Christ.

Rabbi Jesus had to be born by the power of the Holy Spirit so Jesus' blood was not compromised. It is interesting to note that the blood of the fetus and that of the mother never mix during pregnancy. I am convinced that God created the womb of women for Himself, knowing that He was going to use the womb of a woman to bring into our world the promised Messiah, who carried incorruptible blood (see 1 Peter 1:23 KJV). The blood of Jesus Christ is truly precious and was used in the atonement of our soul, silencing the voice of the accuser in the Courts of Heaven.

In fact under the Law almost everything is cleansed with blood, and without the shedding of blood there is no forgiveness [neither release from sin and its guilt, nor cancellation of the merited punishment] (Hebrews 9:22 AMP).

Hebrews 9:22 captures what is known in biblical theology as the "law of redemption." We are told that Rabbi Jesus perfectly fulfilled but did not abolish the Law of Moses. Almost everything is cleansed with blood. Without the shedding of blood there is no forgiveness or atonement for sin. This is a very important law that must be fully appreciated and understood.

The Messiah's blood vanquished sin, hell, and the grave!

The law of redemption puts blood at the heart and center of humanity's cleansing and restoration from the stench and corruption of sin. This law of redemption was acted out a gazillion times in the many animal sacrifices offered by the Levitical priestly order, which foreshadowed the coming of the Messiah, whose blood would vanquish sin, hell, and the grave. This explains why we can use the blood of Jesus in the Courts of Heaven to silence the voice of the accuser. When Rabbi Jesus shed His precious blood on the cross, He triggered the law of redemption throughout human history.

But you have come to Mount Zion and to the city of the living God, the heavenly Jerusalem, and to myriads of angels [in festive gathering], and to the general assembly and assembly of the firstborn who are registered [as citizens] in heaven, and to God, who is Judge of all, and to the spirits of the righteous (the redeemed in heaven) who have been made perfect [bringing them to their final glory] (Hebrews 12:22-23 AMP).

Hebrews 12:22-23 reveals a very powerful list of the voices found in the Courts of Heaven. Based on these two verses, the following are some of those voices:

- The voice of God the Father, who is the Judge of all
- The voice of angels
- The voice of the crowd of witnesses
- The voice of the Advocate (Jesus)
- The voice of the blood of Jesus
- The voice of the accuser (satan)

That list reveals one of the most powerful dimensions in the Spirit that we can step into to manifest breakthrough because Rabbi Jesus graciously redeemed us.

Among the voices in the courts, only one voice is adversarial to the children of God, to us—the voice of the accuser and archenemy of our soul. That means the odds are definitely in our favor to prevail over the devil in the Courts of Heaven when presenting our case before our loving heavenly Father and righteous Judge.

And they overcame and conquered him because of the blood of the Lamb and because of the word of their testimony, for they did not love their life and renounce their faith even when faced with death (Revelation 12:11 AMP).

They overcame and conquered him because of the blood of the Lamb.

Cain killed Abel, and the blood of Abel, unlike the blood of Jesus, was not crying for mercy or forgiveness for Cain—it was crying for vengeance against the horrible murder Cain had committed. The first manifestation of the Courts of Heaven on earth can be traced back to the Garden of Eden when God judged Adam and Eve for the treasonous rebellion. Adam and Eve sinned against God's Kingdom and authority.

The second time the Courts of Heaven manifested on earth was when God visited Cain to interrogate him about the brother he had just killed. During this second trial of the Courts of Heaven on earth, we discover that even the "earth" can be an effective witness against us in the Courts of Heaven.

In my book *Dangerous Prayers from the Courts of Heaven that Destroy Evil Altars,* I wrote an extensive passage on the seven drops of blood that identify the seven places where Rabbi Jesus shed His blood. In summary:

1. Jesus sweat drops of blood in the garden of Gethsemane (see Luke 22:44).

2. Jesus was struck on His face with fists and rods after being arrested (see Matthew 26:63-37).

3. Jesus' beard was pulled out while in custody (see Isaiah 50:5-6).

4. Jesus' back was whipped by the Roman soldiers (see Matthew 27:26).

5. Jesus blood was shed when a crown of thorns was forced into His head before being crucified (see Matthew 27:29).

6. Jesus' hands and feet were impaled with nails as part of the crucifixion (see Matthew 27:35).

7. Jesus' side was pierced with a spear while hanging on the cross (see John 19:34).

When we repent and invoke the precious blood of Jesus, all our sins and transgressions are completely forgiven. They are washed away in the sea of His grace and mercy. This is the clear testimony of the book of 1 John 1:9 (AMP):

> If we [freely] admit that we have sinned and confess our sins, He is faithful and just [true to His own nature and promises], and will forgive our sins and cleanse us continually from all unrighteousness [our wrongdoing, everything not in conformity with His will and purpose].

When we repent and invoke the precious blood of Jesus, all our sins and transgressions are completely forgiven. They are washed away in the sea of His grace and mercy.

Introspection Questions and Scenarios

Leviticus 17:11 (NLT) says, *"for the life of the body is in its blood. I have given you the blood on the altar to purify you, making you right with the Lord. It is the blood, given in exchange for a life, that makes purification possible."* In what way(s) does this Bible version differ from the Amplified Bible or New King James Version? Do they all in essence offer the same truth? Which do you prefer? Why?

_____

_____

_____

_____

_____

_____

_____

Are you, like the author, convinced that God created women's wombs for Himself, knowing that He was going to use a woman's womb to bring into our world His Son, the promised Messiah, who carried incorruptible blood? (See 1 Peter 1:23 KJV.)

_____

_____

_____

_____

_____

_____

_____

Of the five voices heard in the Courts of Heaven, over the past week or so, which one has been the loudest? The faintest? Why is that?

_____

_____

_____

_____

_____

_____

_____

_____

_____

> *And they overcame and conquered him because of the blood of the Lamb and because of the word of their testimony, for they did not love their life and renounce their faith even when faced with death* (Revelation 12:11 AMP).

The odds are definitely in your favor when considering *Who* is on your side in the Courts of Heaven—nevertheless, even when considering all the blood that Jesus shed for you, how certain are you that you will not renounce your faith when faced with death?

_____

_____

_____

_____

_____

_____

_____

_____

Scripture Study and Soul Searching

Prayerfully consider each of the following Scriptures relevant in this session and write your thoughts regarding the blood of Jesus and the Courts of Heaven:

Leviticus 17:11

_____

_____

_____

_____

_____

_____

Romans 3:23

_____

_____

_____

_____

_____

_____

_____

1 Peter 1:23

_____

_____

_____

_____

_____

_____

_____

Hebrews 9:22

_____

_____

_____

_____

_____

_____

_____

Hebrews 12:22-23

_____

_____

_____

_____

_____

_____

_____

Hebrews 12:24

_____

_____

_____

_____

_____

_____

_____

Revelation 12:11

_____

_____

_____

_____

_____

_____

1 John 1:9

_____

_____

_____

_____

_____

_____

Luke 22:44

_____

_____

_____

_____

_____

_____

Genesis 3:17-19

_____

Matthew 26:63-67

_____

Isaiah 50:5-6

_____

Matthew 27:26

_____

_____

_____

_____

_____

_____

_____

Isaiah 53:5

_____

_____

_____

_____

_____

_____

_____

Matthew 27:29

_____

_____

_____

_____

_____

_____

_____

Proverbs 10:15

Matthew 27:35

Psalm 90:17

Psalm 37:23

_____

_____

_____

_____

_____

_____

_____

John 19:34

_____

_____

_____

_____

_____

_____

_____

_____

Activation Application

Take time to research on Biblegateway.com how many times "blood" is mentioned in God's Word. Randomly choose 10 verses or passages of Scripture to write down and then extract the wisdom God is releasing to you from each. Write what you learn.

On a scale from 1 (least) to 10 (most), assess the level of pain for each of the seven times Jesus' human body was subjected to distress and torture and caused His flesh to bleed:

1. _____   Deep anguish and agony while praying (Luke 22:44 AMP)

2. _____   Savagely struck on His face (Matthew 26:63-67 AMP)

3. _____   His beard, facial hair pulled out (Isaiah 50:5-6)

4. _____   His bare back was whipped, flogged (Matthew 27:26 AMP)

5. _____   Sharp thorns shoved into His head (Matthew 27:29 AMP)

6. _____   Large spikes were nailed through His hands and feet (Matthew 27:35 AMP)

7. _____   A spear was thrust into His side (John 19:34 AMP)

How does the reality of Jesus' suffering affect your sense of sacrifice on His part for your redemption?

_____

_____

_____

_____

_____

_____

_____

_____

_____

_____

Reflections and Ruminations

Reflect on a time when you were suffering not only in your body but in your mind, relationships, financially, or otherwise. How "pain tolerant" are you? At the sight of blood do you faint, wince, vomit?

If you were one of those standing near the cross when Jesus was hanging there dripping with blood, what would you do? Run away from Him? Run toward Him? Freeze in place? Sob in desperation?

What would such a scene do to your faith? Strengthen it? Stymie it?

_____

_____

_____

_____

_____

_____

_____

_____

_____

_____

_____

_____

_____

_____

_____

_____

_____

_____

_____

_____

_____

Prayers and Proclamations

Your prayers can absolutely usher you into God's presence in the Courts of Heaven. Upon arriving there, allow the Holy Spirit, your Advocate, to guide you into proclaiming Jesus, the One who redeemed you from hell and set you free.

Heavenly Father, of all the voices in the Courts of Heaven, Yours is the one I yearn to hear. Yours is the one I long to obey. Yours is the one I need to shout in my ear as a still, small voice, the voice of truth and justice. May You continue to mete out freedom from Your throne sprinkled with the precious blood of Jesus. From the first time Your Son, my Advocate, shed blood in the garden of Gethsemane to the last time He shed it on the cross, Your mercy is obvious and Your love is genuine. May I never give You cause to become angry or lose Your favor, dear Lord. I will accept with gratitude all Your gifts and promises so I am prepared to share the Good News of the gospel and advance Your Kingdom on earth as it is in Heaven. Amen and amen, in Jesus' name.

I proclaim, as written in Isaiah 1:18, that although my sins are as scarlet, they are now white as snow!

I declare that God will direct my path in the way of righteous all the days of my life!

I proclaim every evil spirit of accusation will be destroyed in the mighty name of Jesus!

I declare my spiritual growth and God-given productivity potential are operating at optimal capacity!

Session Summary Notes

Successfully Presenting Cases in the Courts of Heaven

Therefore let us [with privilege] approach the throne of grace [that is, the throne of God's gracious favor] with confidence and without fear, so that we may receive mercy [for our failures] and find [His amazing] grace to help in time of need [an appropriate blessing, coming just at the right moment] (Hebrews 4:16 AMP).

Two of the most frequently asked questions by people who discover the Courts of Heaven are: "How do I present my case in the Courts of Heaven?" and, "Is there a spiritual and established protocol for presenting cases in the Courts of Heaven?" Thankfully for us, the Bible does not leave us any option to second-guess how to make our approach before God. Now I share with you how to present your cases effectively and successfully in the Courts of Heaven.

Come now, and let us reason together!

In Isaiah 41:21, the Lord encourages us to present our case before Him, and in the process bring forth our strong reasons or evidence for why we deserve a righteous verdict in our favor from our righteous Judge.

"Come now, and let us reason together," says the Lord, *"though your sins are like scarlet, they shall be as white as snow; though they are red like crimson, they shall be as wool"* (Isaiah 1:18 NKJV).

The following are eight important ways to prepare yourself and get ready to present your case in the Courts of Heaven:

1. *Get off the battlefield.* There is a spiritual battle between good and evil (see Ephesians 6:12), and we must not only arm ourselves with the full armor of God, we must also recognize the legal precedents set forth in the Courts of Heaven.

2. *Ask for the Courts of Heaven to be seated.* Before approaching the Courts of Heaven, ask that the Courts of Heaven be seated to hear and adjudicate your case. We make this request in and through the mighty name of Jesus Christ our Savior and Lord. It's impossible to get a judicial ruling if the court is not seated to hear the case. When you have a confirmation in your spirit that the Court is seated to hear your case,

start presenting your case in faith. (See Daniel 7:10 NKJV.)

3. *Stand on Christ's finished work of the cross.* Realize that approaching the Courts of Heaven must be based on the finished work of Christ on the cross (see John 19:28-30). Without this substitutionary work of our Savior, we don't qualify to approach our holy God's courts. Quoting Scriptures of Christ's sacrifice on the cross gives us stature as we present our cases and gives us an advantage over the accuser.

4. *Repent!* Ask the Holy Spirit to search your heart and see if there is any unconfessed sin in your life. Repentance is at the heart of entering the Kingdom (see Matthew 4:17). Repentance resets your relationship with God and gives you a favorable standing in the Courts of Heaven.

5. *Present your case with boldness.* When approaching the Courts of Heaven, do so in a spirit of boldness, not fear. *"Let us therefore come boldly to the throne of grace, that we may obtain mercy and find grace to help in time of need"* (Hebrews 4:16 NKJV). Fear works against us and gives our chief adversary legal footing against us in the Courts of Heaven.

6. *Wait for the Holy Spirit's witness.* While presenting your case in the Courts of Heaven, wait for the witness of the Holy Spirit before leaving the courtroom. The Holy Spirit is the highest Officer of the Courts of Heaven, and He will you give a witness in your spirit when the righteous verdict you're seeking has been granted. If it has not been granted, ask Him

why and He's faithful to answer you promptly because all of Heaven wants to answer your prayers. *"The Spirit Himself bears witness with our spirit that we are children of God"* (Romans 8:16 NKJV). The Bible says as many as are *"led by the Holy Spirit they are children of God"* (Romans 8:14 NKJV). So being led by the Holy Spirit in the Courts of Heaven is an absolute must.

7. *Receive the Court's verdict by faith.* Your accuser can only prevent the Courts of Heaven from rendering a righteous verdict on your behalf because he still has legal grounds to do so. Ask the Holy Spirit to show you what is in satan's evidence docket so you can render it useless by repenting and invoking the blood of Jesus. Then receive your righteous verdict by faith (see John 8:10-11 NKJV).

8. *Reinforce your righteous verdict daily through thanksgiving.* One of our most powerful weapons is thanksgiving, which places us in an attitude of continual praise over what the Lord has already done for us. Thanksgiving is so powerful that God has made it His direct will for all of His children (see 1 Thessalonians 5:28). Thanksgiving feeds our spirit with hopeful anticipation and expectancy—that's when miracles happen. When you receive the Holy Spirit's "witness" that the divine restraining order you requested against your accuser has been granted, maintain an attitude of thanksgiving.

Introspection Questions and Scenarios

After reading the book and (almost) completing this study guide, what are your answers to the two questions asked at the beginning of this session:

1. "How do I present my case in the Courts of Heaven?"

_____

_____

_____

2. "Is there a spiritual and established protocol for presenting cases in the Courts of Heaven?"

_____

_____

_____

When it comes to battling your adversary, are you at times too quick to jump into your armor and wield your sword rather than stopping to consider what actual legal evidence he has against you in the Courts of Heaven?

_____

_____

_____

_____

The judge in the earthly courts must be seated before the trial proceedings can begin. Likewise in the Courts of Heaven the eternal Judge must be seated before your Advocate can present your case. How will you know when God is seated? Who will signal that your case is now being presented?

_____

_____

_____

_____

Because quoting Scriptures on the finished work of Christ on the cross gives us stature and an advantage over the accuser in the heavenly court, write down all the Scriptures that the Holy Spirit brings to your mind. Then determine to memorize all, or at least a few, to have ready to quote during your trial(s).

_____

_____

_____

_____

_____

_____

_____

_____

_____

_____

_____

_____

_____

_____

_____

Some hyper-grace followers believe they only need to repent once—as if born-again believers are incapable of sinning against God in their body of flesh. Nothing could be further from the truth. What does repenting mean to you and how often is repentance necessary to maintain a right relationship with God and a favorable standing in the Courts of Heaven?

_____

_____

_____

_____

_____

_____

_____

_____

_____

When considering standing before the heavenly courts, are you bold or fearful? How does knowing your Advocate is standing with you alter that feeling of fear?

In an earthly courtroom, would the defendant and attorney leave the room without knowing the verdict? No. Neither should you leave until the Holy Spirit gives you a witness in your spirit that a righteous verdict has been granted. Are you guilty of rushing out of the courtroom to get on with your life before being led by the Spirit?

You will not get a physical piece of paper stating your righteous verdict from the Courts of Heaven's Judge. But a verdict rendered in Heaven is more real and consequential than any verdict rendered by a natural court of law. How does your faith enter into this final verdict?

Is thanking God for His many blessings and interventions and saving grace part of your daily interactions with Him? Why or why not?

_____

_____

_____

_____

_____

_____

_____

_____

_____

_____

_____

_____

_____

_____

_____

_____

_____

_____

_____

_____

_____

_____

_____

_____

_____

_____

_____

Scripture Study and Soul Searching

Prayerfully consider each of the following Scriptures relevant in this session and write your thoughts regarding how to successfully present your case(s) in the Courts of Heaven:

Isaiah 41:21

Isaiah 1:18

Luke 18:1-8

Daniel 7:10

_____

_____

_____

_____

_____

_____

John 19:28-30

_____

_____

_____

_____

_____

_____

Matthew 4:17

_____

_____

_____

_____

_____

_____

Hebrews 4:16

1 John 4:18

Romans 8:16

Romans 8:14

_____

_____

_____

_____

_____

_____

John 8:10-11

_____

_____

_____

_____

_____

_____

_____

1 Thessalonians 5:18

_____

_____

_____

_____

_____

_____

_____

Activation Application

Assess your circumstances right now regarding your work life, home life, and spiritual life. Is there any aspect of your life that the accuser can bring charges against you in the Courts of Heaven? Which of the ways will you use to successfully present your case in the courtroom?

_____

_____

_____

_____

_____

_____

_____

_____

_____

_____

With your ever-faithful Advocate beside you when presenting your case, how hard will it be for you to be bold and confident yet humble and gracious before your righteous Judge?

_____

_____

_____

_____

_____

_____

_____

_____

_____

_____

Reflections and Ruminations

"Present your case," says the Lord. "Bring forth your strong reasons," says the King of Jacob (Isaiah 41:21 NKJV).

In Isaiah 41:21, the Lord encourages you to present your case before Him, and in the process bring forth your strong reasons or evidence for why you deserve a righteous verdict in your favor from your righteous Judge. And in Isaiah 1:18 the Lord says:

"Come now, and let us reason together," says the Lord, "though your sins are like scarlet, they shall be as white as snow; though they are red like crimson, they shall be as wool" (Isaiah 1:18 NKJV).

Picture yourself sitting in your living room with your Advocate reasoning together and discussing your case and what is involved in the proceedings. Do the charges have a legal basis? Will you or your Advocate confront the accusations against you before the Judge? As the defendant, how engaged are you in the process? Does your Advocate handle all the detail work? Will He call witnesses to the stand who can confirm your innocence? How vocal will your accuser be in the courtroom? Will hearing his threats against you affect your defense? Will you tell the truth, the whole truth, and nothing but the truth? How confident are you that the Advocate will give you the help you need when you need it in the Courts of Heaven?

_____

_____

_____

_____

_____

_____

_____

_____

_____

_____

But when the Father sends the Advocate as my representative—that is, the Holy Spirit— he will teach you everything and will remind you of everything I have told you (John 14:26 NLT).

Prayers and Proclamations

Your prayers can absolutely usher you into God's presence in the Courts of Heaven. Upon arriving there, allow the Holy Spirit, your Advocate, to guide you into proclaiming Jesus, the One who redeemed you from hell and set you free.

Oh righteous Judge, thank You for opening the doors to the Courts of Heaven and hearing my case. I praise You and am so very grateful that You sent the Holy Spirit to my aid and that the Advocate will be right beside me when I enter Your courtroom. As the court is seated and the trial begins, I pray, Lord, that all present will see Your glory and majesty and know that You are the one and only righteous Judge, ever ruling in favor of Your children. I will present the truth of Your Word that I have been redeemed by the shed blood of Jesus on the cross. I pray that You will rule in my favor, not because I'm deserving but because Your Son made the ultimate sacrifice for my sins. I repent of whatever sins the Holy Spirit brings to my attention. I sincerely want to please You, God, with my obedience, praise, and worship. Have mercy on me, dear heavenly Father, in Jesus' name, amen.

I proclaim victory over my enemies because my Advocate presented my case before the righteous Judge of Heaven and earth!

I declare that the blood of Jesus erases every evil accusation against me!

I proclaim that the Courts of Heaven recognize me as a child of God and release me from every curse ever said over me!

I declare that my righteous verdict of release and breakthrough has shut the gates of hell and opened the gates of Heaven!

Session Summary Notes

About the Author

Dr. Francis Myles is a multi-gifted international motivational speaker, business consultant, and apostle to the nations. He is the senior pastor of Dream Genesis Church International in Lusaka, Zambia, and Franklin, Tennessee. He is also the creator and founder of the world's first *Marketplace Bible.* He is a sought-after conference speaker in both ministerial and marketplace seminars. Dr. Myles is also a spiritual life coach to movers and shakers in the marketplace and political arena. He has appeared on TBN, GodTV, and Daystar. He has been a featured guest on Sid Roth's *It's Supernatural!* TV show. Dr. Myles is happily married to the love of his life, Carmela Real Myles, and they have an office and studios in Atlanta Metroplex in the state of Georgia.

Contact Information

Website: FrancisMyles.com

Francis Myles International
950 Eagle's Landing Parkway
Unit 608
Stockbridge, GA 30281

Phone: 404-870-7017

Email: support@francismyles.com